SECRETS OF OUTDOOR SURVIVAL SKILLS FOR KIDS REVEALED

LEARN HOW TO MAKE A FIRE, BUILD A SHELTER, FIND WATER AND OTHER SKILLS TO SURVIVE THE WILDERNESS

BRENT MARSHALL

CONTENTS

INTRODUCTION

You're on a family hike in the woods. The sun is setting, and you realize you've wandered off the trail. You look around and see nothing but trees. Panic starts to set in. What do you do? This book is here to help you answer that question. It's packed with skills and tips to help you stay safe and find your way back.

The purpose of this book is simple: to teach you outdoor survival skills in a way that's easy to understand and fun to learn. These skills are important. They can keep you safe and help you feel more confident in nature. They can even help you connect more deeply with the world around you.

This book is written just for kids like you. It's perfect if you're between 5 and 10 years old. It's both educational and entertaining. You'll learn a lot, and you'll have fun doing it.

Here's what you'll find inside:

- **First Aid**: Basic skills to treat cuts, bruises, and other common injuries.
- **Making a Fire**: Safe ways to build a fire for warmth and cooking.
- **Building a Shelter**: How to make a shelter to protect yourself from the elements.
- **Finding Water**: Tips on finding and purifying water to drink.
- **Foraging**: Identifying and collecting edible plants.
- **Navigation Skills**: Using a map and compass to find your way.
- **Weather Awareness**: Understanding weather patterns to stay safe.
- **Survival Mindset**: Staying calm and thinking clearly in challenging situations.

This book also includes real-life stories of kids who have used these skills to survive. These stories will show you that you can do it, too.

Safety is our top priority. All the advice in this book is safe and accurate. We won't tell you to do anything dangerous or hard to understand. We focus on practical skills that you can use in many different places. There are some things we won't cover. We won't talk about advanced tactical skills or information specific to certain regions. We focus on practical, safe outdoor survival knowledge suitable for all readers. This book is all about giving you practical, general survival knowledge. There are topics we will cover that may seem stressful or scary. We will cover what you should do if you need to be rescued. This book is not meant to put you in a situation where you need help or rescuing. But that doesn't mean it won't happen. If you or your group ever winds up in a bad situation needing rescuing, the skills in this book will help you know what to do.

Let me introduce myself. I'm passionate about helping kids overcome outdoor challenges. I aim for you to discover a sense of independence and foster a deep connection with the natural world around you. Through years of exploring the wilderness and mastering survival techniques, I've gathered a wealth of knowledge and experience. It's this expertise that I'm eager to share with you, offering clear, straightforward guidance that's easy for young adventurers to understand and apply. Whether you're navigating through dense forests or identifying safe, edible plants, I'm here to ensure your journey into outdoor survival is both educational and empowering.

The book is organized into chapters, each focusing on a specific skill. You'll begin by mastering the fundamental skills, gradually progressing to more complex techniques as you grow more confident in your abilities. As you journey through this book, you'll find that each chapter acts as a steppingstone to the next, deepening your understanding and skills in outdoor survival as you progress, so you'll always be learning something new.

This book is not just a resource for young adventurers; it can be a vital tool for everyone you know. Parents, guardians, siblings, and friends can join the learning journey, turning each skill into an engaging group activity. This collaborative approach is fantastic for strengthening bonds, creating lasting memories, and ensuring everyone has crucial survival skills. Picture setting up a practice camp in your backyard, where family members take turns trying to spark a fire with the newly learned techniques or plan a group hike to test your navigational abilities. These activities enhance the learning experience by fostering teamwork and the thrill of shared accomplishments.

Learning outdoor survival skills is an adventure. It's a chance to explore and have fun in nature. You'll feel more confident and prepared for anything. So let's get started. Nature is waiting for you.

CHAPTER ONE
GETTING STARTED WITH OUTDOOR SURVIVAL

After reading this book, imagine you're on an adventure in the woods with your family. You realize you and your family strayed from the path during your exploration. An endless sea of trees surrounds you. As the sun begins to set, you start to wonder if you'll make it back to safety before nightfall, and a wave of panic washes over you. However, the panic disappears because you recall the valuable skills you've read in this book. You're equipped to handle this with knowledge like how to remain calm, build a shelter, and make a fire. This book is crafted to arm you with these and other skills, so you know you're prepared to survive in the wilderness.

UNDERSTANDING SURVIVAL BASICS

Survival skills are important for anyone who spends time outdoors. They help you stay safe, build confidence, and become more independent. Knowing how to handle different situations, you can explore nature without fear. These skills are life skills that you can use in many areas of your life. For example, knowing how to make a fire can help you during a camping trip. Understanding how to find clean water can be helpful if you ever face an emergency. These skills give you the tools to care for yourself and help others.

The four basic needs for survival are shelter, water, fire, and food. Shelter keeps you safe from the weather. A shelter can protect you and keep you warm if it's raining, snowing, or very windy. Water is necessary for your body to function. You need to stay hydrated to stay healthy and strong. Fire can keep you warm, cook food, and signal for help. It's one of the most important survival tools. Food gives you the energy to keep going. Knowing how to find and prepare food can make a big difference in a survival situation.

Having the right mindset is also very important in survival situations. Staying calm and positive can help you think clearly and make good decisions. When you panic, it's hard to focus and solve problems. But if you stay calm, you can figure out what to do next. Maintaining a positive outlook is crucial for pushing through challenging times, and staying positive fuels your motivation and determination, shining like a light in difficult times. A positive attitude isn't just about feeling good; it's a powerful tool for survival. In the wilderness, where uncertainty looms large, maintaining a positive outlook can erase the shadows of panic, allowing you to discover solutions and opportunities. History is filled with remarkable survival stories of individuals who faced seemingly impossible odds, overcame their fear, and kept going. They knew that giving up was not an option. By maintaining a positive attitude, they used their knowledge of survival and came up with creative strategies to ensure their safety. This kind of resilience and positive thinking can transform a bad situation into a story of survival.

Safety is the most important part of any survival activity. Making safety your top priority is fundamental to every outdoor adventure and survival situation. It's crucial to exercise caution and good judgment, not taking actions that could expose you to unnecessary risks. This means avoiding shortcuts through unknown or hazardous terrain, steering clear of wildlife, and not taking chances with extreme weather. Every decision should be made with safety in mind, ensuring that your adventure isn't dangerous. Remember, the wilderness demands respect, and by avoiding risky behaviors, you're showing that you understand and honor this principle.

Embrace the buddy system as a cornerstone of outdoor safety. Whenever you venture into the wilderness or practice your survival skills, ensure a friend or a family member accompanies you. This partnership serves as a mutual support network, allowing both of you to watch out for one another in case any challenges arise. By sharing the journey, you are safer with your buddy and also sharing the learning experience, as two heads are often better than one when solving problems or making critical decisions. This collaborative approach ensures that should an unexpected situation occur, you have immediate assistance and can jointly devise a plan to overcome any obstacle.

Always communicate your plans to someone you trust. Before embarking on any outdoor adventure, it's crucial to inform a family member, friend, or park ranger about your destination, the route you plan to take, and your expected return time. By providing these details, if you do not return as scheduled, they'll know where to direct search and rescue efforts. This simple step can significantly increase your chances of being found quickly in an emergency. Also, consider leaving a note or a map with your planned route highlighted. This level of preparedness ensures that, even if plans change, those looking for you have a solid starting point.

Survival is not just about knowing the skills. It's about using them safely and wisely. Whether building a shelter, making a fire, or finding water, always consider safety first. These skills are tools that can help you in many ways. They can keep you safe, build your confidence, and help you connect with nature.

THE IMPORTANCE OF PREPARATION AND PLANNING

Preparation is vital when it comes to outdoor survival. Being well-prepared means you can handle unexpected situations more easily. It prevents many problems before they even start. Think of it like doing your homework before a big test. You wouldn't walk into a test without studying. The same goes for heading into the wilderness. When you plan your trip, you're setting yourself up for success. Checking the weather forecast is a good start. Knowing what to expect helps you pack the right gear. If it's going to rain, you'll need a rain jacket. If it's going to be hot, you'll need extra water. Informing someone about your plans is also crucial. Let a friend or family member know where you're going and when you'll be back. This way, they'll know where to look for you if something happens.

Let's break down the steps for effective planning. First, choose a safe location. Pick a place that's suitable for your skill level. If you're new to hiking, start with a well-marked trail. Avoid areas with dangerous wildlife or rugged terrain. Next, create a packing checklist. Write down everything you need to bring. This includes food, water, clothing, and survival gear. Having a checklist ensures you don't forget anything important. Planning your route is the next step. Study the map and decide which path you'll take. Note any landmarks or points of interest along the way. This helps you stay on track and avoid getting lost.

Knowing your environment is another crucial part of preparation. Research the area you'll be exploring. Learn about the local plants and animals. This knowledge can help you identify edible plants or avoid dangerous ones. For example, knowing what poison ivy looks like can save you from an itchy rash. Understanding the terrain is also helpful. Are there steep hills or rocky paths? Knowing this in advance helps you prepare mentally and physically. Recognizing potential hazards is crucial. Are there areas prone to flooding? Is the path known for having loose rocks? Being aware of these risks helps you navigate safely.

Practice makes perfect. Regular practice builds ability and confidence. Before you head out, practice your survival skills at home. After you read Chapter 3: Fire Making Techniques, you'll be ready to prepare everything you need to be safe, gather some dry tinder and kindling, and practice starting a fire in a secure location and under adult supervision. Some of the fire-making techniques will require practice to get just right. After you read Chapter 4: Building a Shelter, you'll be ready to try building a practice shelter. Using gear like a tarp and rope to build a shelter will allow you to test your gear before you go on an adventure. After you read Chapter 7: Navigational Skills, you'll be ready to start using a map and compass to find your way around a local park. These activities make the skills second nature, so they're ready when you need them.

When you're prepared, you can handle almost anything the wilderness throws at you. Preparation serves as your adventure's safety net. It gives you the tools and knowledge to stay safe and enjoy your time outdoors. So, before you head out on your next adventure, take the time to plan and prepare. It's worth it.

ESSENTIAL SURVIVAL GEAR

When you venture into the great outdoors, having the right gear can make all the difference. Let's start by looking at some must-have survival items. A multi-tool or Swiss army knife is an indispensable companion for any young adventurer venturing into the great outdoors. These compact gadgets have various tools, including a sharp knife, scissors, and a versatile screwdriver. With these at your disposal, you're well-prepared to handle multiple tasks: slicing through ropes, opening canned goods, or carving sticks into useful shapes and tools. However, exercising caution and respect towards these tools is always important. Make sure you're familiar with the proper use of each function, handling each part of the multi-tool with care to avoid accidents. Safety should always be your top priority, making sure that every adventure remains fun and injury-free.

A first-aid kit is an absolute must-have for any young explorer. Your kit should be stocked with various size bandages for different wounds, antiseptic wipes to clean cuts and prevent infection, and tweezers for safely removing splinters or ticks. Additionally, include a few packets of antibiotic ointment to apply on scratches to keep them clean and sting relief pads for those pesky bug bites. Understanding how to use each component of your first-aid kit properly is crucial. For instance, knowing how to apply pressure to a wound with a bandage can control bleeding, while using antiseptic wipes correctly can prevent infections before they start. Knowing how to use all the items in your first-aid kit can help you treat minor injuries quickly and prevent any injuries from escalating into more severe issues.

Fire-starting tools are a critical component of your survival gear. Having a reliable means to start a fire can be a game-changer in the wilderness. Essential fire-starting tools include waterproof matches, a durable lighter, and flint and steel. Flint and steel, in particular, stand out for their reliability under adverse conditions, as they can generate sparks even when wet, making them an invaluable tool for any young explorer. A well-built fire provides essential warmth on cold nights, reducing the risk of hypothermia. It also serves as a cooking heat source, allowing you to boil water to make it safe to drink and cook any food you might have. Additionally, a fire can be a signal for help, visible from far away, increasing your chances of rescue.

On any adventure, a compass and map can become your best friends, guiding you through unknown territories with confidence. These tools are essential for any young adventurer, ensuring you can always find your way, even when the path ahead seems uncertain. Learning to read a map isn't just about recognizing landmarks; it's about understanding the language of the land – where rivers flow, how mountains rise, and where valleys fall. Pairing this knowledge with a compass, which points you in the right direction, lets you navigate any terrain easily. Using a compass alongside a map requires practice. Still, it is a skill that can improve your outdoor adventures. Start by familiarizing yourself with the compass's basic functions: finding north, aligning the compass with your map, and setting a course. Once you've mastered these steps, you're on your way to becoming a proficient navigator. Remember, the key to successful navigation is patience and precision. Take time to correctly align your map and compass, ensuring your bearings are accurate. This careful approach will help you reach your destination and be helpful if you become lost and must trace your steps back to safety.

Selecting the appropriate gear is important for your adventures outdoors. Choose items that are not only functional but also lightweight and compact. Carrying heavy or bulky equipment can slow you down, making you feel weighed down and exhausted faster than expected. It's essential to balance how much you need each item and how much each item weighs, making sure that each piece of gear serves a purpose without becoming a burden. Remember, the key is to travel smart, carrying only what you need to remain agile and energetic throughout your journey. Look for age-appropriate tools that are simple to use but effective. Make sure your gear is durable and reliable. You don't want something that breaks easily when you need it the most. For example, choose a multi-tool made from stainless steel. It's solid and resistant to rust. When selecting a first-aid kit, pick one that's compact but includes all the basics. A small, well-stocked kit is easier to carry and still provides what you need.

Taking care of your gear ensures it lasts a long time. Clean and dry your tools after each use. This keeps your gear in good condition. Regularly check your gear for wear and tear. If you see any damage, repair it right away. Proper storage is also important. Keep your gear in a dry, cool place. Store your multi-tool in its case. Keep your first-aid kit in a waterproof bag. This protects it from moisture and dirt. Make sure your fire-starting tools are dry and stored in a safe place. A small, waterproof container works well for matches and lighters.

Understanding the purpose and use of each item in your survival kit can boost your confidence. Knowing you have the right tools makes you feel more prepared for any situation. This confidence can help you stay calm and think clearly. Always remember to handle your gear with care. Safety should always come first. Follow these tips, and you'll be ready for your next adventure in the great outdoors.

CREATING YOUR OWN BUG OUT BAG

A bug-out bag is a backpack filled with needed items in an emergency. Imagine you're on a camping trip and a sudden storm forces you to leave your campsite quickly. A bug-out bag means you can grab it and go, knowing you have what you need to stay safe and comfortable. It's all about being ready for anything, whether a quick evacuation or an unexpected night in the woods. Emergency preparedness is vital. With your bug-out bag, you'll be prepared to face any situation confidently.

Let's look at what you should include in your bug-out bag. In the last section, we discussed multi-tools, a first-aid kit, fire-starting tools, compasses, and maps. These should all go in your bug-out bag. In Chapter 4: Building a Shelter, we'll talk about how to build a shelter with a tarp, strong rope, and tent stakes. Pack these materials in your bag to be prepared to make a shelter. In Chapter 5: Finding and Purifying Water, we'll discuss how to find drinkable water. If you have any equipment for collecting water, that equipment should also go in your bug-out bag. Next, pack non-perishable snacks. These foods, like granola bars, dried fruit, and trail mix, won't spoil quickly. They'll give you energy when you need it most. Next, pack extra clothing layers. Think about the weather and pack accordingly. Include a warm jacket, a hat, and gloves for cold weather. Pack a lightweight shirt and a hat for sun protection in warmer climates. Personal hygiene items are also important. Pack a small toothbrush, toothpaste, wet wipes, and hand sanitizer. Staying clean can keep you healthy and comfortable. An emergency whistle is another must-have. It's a simple tool that can make a lot of noise to signal for help if you get lost or need assistance.

Now, what's the best way to pack your bug-out bag? If you have a bag with multiple compartments or pouches, use those to organize your items. This way, you can quickly find what you need without emptying the entire bag. For example, keep your snacks in one compartment and your hygiene items in another. It's also very important to make sure the weight of the items in your bug-out bag is balanced evenly. A well-packed bag allows you to move freely and efficiently, avoiding unnecessary strain on your back or shoulders. Aim to place heavier items towards the bottom and closer to your spine, where your body can handle the weight more effectively. Lighter items should be packed on top and in the outer compartments. This strategy makes your bag easier to carry, keeps it stable, and prevents it from shifting as you move. Periodically adjust and test the arrangement of items in your bag to find the most comfortable setup for your body, ensuring that the load is evenly distributed and doesn't pull you backward or to one side. This thoughtful approach to packing will significantly enhance your ability to carry your bug-out bag for extended periods of time over long distances or up steep trails. Strive for a balance that feels right and allows you to move freely and efficiently on your adventures.

MAINTAINING YOUR BUG OUT BAG IS JUST AS IMPORTANT AS CREATING IT

Rotating the food and water supplies means everything is fresh and safe to consume. Over time, even non-perishable food items can degrade in quality or start tasting weird. Water in plastic containers stored in a warm or hot location for extended periods might become contaminated by the container degrading or breaking down, even if the container is sealed. To avoid this, set a schedule to check the expiration dates of all edible items and the water in your bag every few months. If any food is nearing its expiration date, replace it with fresh supplies on your next grocery trip. Consider using commercial bottled water with a known shelf-life or filling durable, clean containers with tap water and replacing them every six months. This practice ensures that your bug-out bag is always ready with consumable, nutritious food and clean water. Still, it also allows you to review and refresh the bag's contents regularly, keeping everything up-to-date and in perfect condition for any emergency.

Updating your clothing with the changing seasons is important for staying comfortable and safe during your adventures. As winter approaches, it's important to pack extra layers of warm clothing in your bug-out bag. Consider including a thermal base layer, a fleece for insulation, and a waterproof outer layer to protect against snow and rain. Don't forget warm socks, a hat, and gloves to prevent heat loss from your extremities. As spring and summer arrive, replace these items with lighter clothing to help you stay cool. Opt for breathable fabrics that wick away moisture, and include a lightweight, long-sleeved shirt to shield you from the sun's rays. A wide-brimmed hat and sunglasses can also protect against sunburn and glare. By matching your emergency wardrobe to the season, you ensure you're always prepared to face the elements, whatever the weather may bring.

Regularly inspect your first-aid kit to ensure all items are within their use-by dates. Expired products may not work effectively when you need them the most, sometimes preventing you from being able to handle minor injuries swiftly. To keep your first-aid kit in top condition, establish a routine to check the expiration dates of antiseptic wipes, antibiotic ointments, and any medications. Replace expired items immediately. This proactive approach guarantees your first-aid kit remains a reliable resource for addressing scrapes, cuts, and other common outdoor injuries.

A bug-out bag is like having a backup plan. It gives you peace of mind knowing you're prepared. Whether it's a sudden storm, getting lost, or having to leave quickly, your bug-out bag has you covered. Keep it in a place where you can grab it easily. Make sure it's packed and maintained so you're always ready and can enjoy your outdoor adventures knowing you're prepared for anything.

CHAPTER TWO
SAFETY FIRST

I magine you're exploring a beautiful forest with your friends. You're having a great time, but suddenly, one of your friends trips and falls. They get a nasty cut on their knee. What do you do? Knowing basic first aid can make a big difference. It helps you take care of injuries until you can get more help. First aid skills become even more important when you're out in nature, far from doctors and hospitals. They can help you treat minor cuts and scrapes, handle insect bites, and manage blisters, sunburns, and dehydration.

HOW TO TREAT COMMON PROBLEMS IN THE WILDERNESS

When you or a friend gets a minor cut or scrape while adventuring outdoors, the first thing you should do is clean the wound. This is a crucial step to prevent infection and make sure the wound heals properly. Begin by cleaning your hands with hand sanitizer. This step is important to avoid spreading germs and bacteria from your hands into the wound. Next, gently rinse the wound with clean water to wash away any dirt or debris that might be inside. Avoid using river or lake water directly on the wound, as it may contain bacteria or other harmful organisms. If there is not enough or no clean water available, you may have to skip rinsing the wound. Even though you can use hand sanitizer to clean your hands, never use hand sanitizer to clean an open wound. Next, use an antiseptic wipe around the edges of the cut or scrape. This helps to kill any bacteria lurking around the wound, reducing the risk of infection. Be careful not to apply too much pressure or cause further irritation to the injury. Once the wound is clean and treated with antiseptic, it's time to protect it with a sterile bandage. Choose a bandage large enough to cover the entire wound, ensuring the adhesive parts do not touch the injury. The bandage should be snug to keep dirt out and absorb any oozing but not so tight that it impedes circulation. If the wound bleeds through the bandage, add another layer instead of removing the first one, which could reopen the wound. Remember, as soon as you get to a location with more medical supplies, you should take another look at the wound to see if it needs to be treated again.

Insect bites and stings are common when you're outdoors. They can be annoying and sometimes even painful. If you or a friend gets stung, the first thing to check is if the stinger is still in the skin. If the stinger is still in the skin, you need to remove it. Doing this with care is important to avoid squeezing more venom into the wound. Ideally, use a pair of tweezers for precision—gently grasp the stinger close to the skin's surface and pull it straight out to minimize irritation. Once the stinger is out, cleaning the area thoroughly is crucial to prevent infection. Use clean water and clean fabric to wash around the sting site, being gentle to avoid further irritation. After cleaning, if the sting feels itchy, make sure the skin is dry and apply some anti-itch cream to the area that was stung.

Blisters from hiking can be painful and make it hard to walk. To treat a blister, start by cleaning the area with clean water. If the blister is small and not too painful, it may be best to leave it alone after washing it. It's very important that you don't pop the blister. Leaving the skin intact will help prevent bacteria and germs from getting into the blister. Cover the blister with a bandage to protect it from rubbing against your clothes or other surfaces.

Sprained ankles are a frequent mishap during outdoor adventures. If you have a twisted ankle, stopping and rest immediately is important. Don't put any weight on the ankle to prevent further injury. Elevate the injured ankle above heart level, if possible, using a backpack, a rock, or any elevated surface nearby. This elevation assists in minimizing swelling by reducing blood flow to the injured area. If you have an elastic bandage in your first-aid kit or bag, carefully wrap it around the ankle. Start from the base of the toes, moving upwards towards the leg to ensure even pressure and support. The bandage should be snug but not too tight, allowing slight movement without restricting blood circulation. This supportive wrapping is crucial for stabilizing the ankle, aiding the healing process, and preventing additional injury as you return to safety.

Sunburns can happen quickly, especially on sunny days. If you get sunburned, move to a shaded area right away. Avoid applying lotions or creams to the sunburn unless they're specifically for sunburn relief. If you have a large hat and extra clothing in your bag, put those on to cover the sunburn. If you don't have extra coverings, consider staying in shaded areas while the sun moves through the sky to reduce the risk of worsening sunburn.

Dehydration can sneak up on you, especially when you're active. Symptoms of dehydration include feeling very thirsty, having a dry mouth, and feeling dizzy or lightheaded. If you think you're dehydrated, stop and rest in a cool, shaded area. You should start to rehydrate in the right way. Start by taking small, steady sips of water instead of gulping down a large amount all at once. Drinking too quickly can overwhelm your system, possibly leading to stomach cramps or nausea, which could make your situation worse. Instead, sip water slowly. This allows your body to absorb the fluid gradually, helping to restore your hydration levels more effectively.

Having a well-stocked first-aid kit is crucial. It should include adhesive bandages of various sizes for cuts and blisters. Tweezers help remove splinters and stingers. Anti-itch cream helps soothe insect bites. Elastic bandages can be used to wrap sprained joints. Other useful items include antiseptic wipes, sterile gauze pads, and a small pair of scissors. Keep your first-aid kit in a waterproof container to protect it from the elements. Make sure everyone in your group knows where it is and how to use the items inside.

First aid is all about being prepared and knowing what to do in an emergency. It helps you stay calm and take action when someone gets hurt. With these skills, you can enjoy outdoor adventures, knowing you're ready for anything.

SAFETY PRECAUTIONS IN THE WILDERNESS

When you venture into the wilderness, following some basic safety rules to avoid accidents and injuries is essential.

We already talked about the buddy system in Chapter 1. But it's so important that we need to go over it again. The buddy system is a crucial part of staying safe in the wilderness. Always have a buddy with you when you explore. This way, you can help each other in case of an emergency. If one of you gets hurt, the other can go for help. Keeping track of each other's whereabouts is also easier with a buddy. You can make sure no one gets lost or separated from the group. Sharing responsibilities makes the adventure more enjoyable and manageable. You can take turns carrying supplies, setting up camp, or cooking meals. Working together makes everything easier and more fun.

Always stay on marked trails. These paths are created to keep you safe and help you avoid getting lost. They also protect the natural environment by preventing damage to plants and wildlife. Avoid wandering into dangerous areas, such as cliffs or fast-moving water. These places can be very risky, and slipping or getting swept away is easy. Hazardous terrain, such as loose rocks and slippery slopes, can lead to falls and injuries. Always watch where you step and take your time on tricky paths.

Encountering poisonous plants such as poison ivy, poison oak, or poison sumac is a common hazard in many outdoor environments. These plants can cause itchy, uncomfortable rashes upon contact with your skin. Recognizing and avoiding these plants is essential for your safety while exploring the wilderness. Poison ivy typically has three shiny green leaves with a red stem, and it can grow as a bush or vine. Poison oak also has leaves in sets of three, but they resemble oak leaves and may have a fuzzy texture. Poison sumac is a bit different, with 7 to 13 leaves on each stem, and it usually grows as a shrub or small tree. All these plants can cause allergic reactions, so if you see plants that match these descriptions, keeping a safe distance is best. These aren't the only types of dangerous plants, so consider learning about the local plant life before going on your next adventure.

Applying insect repellent is crucial in protecting yourself from bites and stings when you're exploring the great outdoors. Mosquitoes and ticks aren't just annoying; they can also be carriers of serious diseases like Lyme disease and West Nile virus. To keep these pests at bay, choose a repellent that's effective against a wide range of biting insects and apply it according to the instructions on the package. Remember to reapply as necessary, especially if you're sweating a lot or if you get wet. For added protection, consider wearing long sleeves and pants, and tuck your pants into your socks or shoes to prevent ticks from crawling up your legs.

Always keep a safe distance from wildlife. Animals may look cute and friendly but can be unpredictable and sometimes dangerous. Enjoy watching them from afar without disturbing their natural behavior. Dangerous animals, such as snakes and bears, are best avoided. If you see a snake, give it plenty of space. If you encounter a bear, stay calm and slowly back away while making yourself look as large as possible. Never run or turn your back on a bear.

Wearing the right clothing and gear is vital for staying safe and comfortable outdoors. Dress in layers to regulate your body temperature. You can add or remove layers as needed to keep warm or cool. Sturdy footwear is also essential. Hiking boots or sturdy shoes provide support and protect your feet from rough terrain. Avoid wearing open-toed sandals or flimsy shoes that can easily get damaged.

Let's look at some examples of proper clothing and gear for different conditions. On a cold day, you might wear a base layer of thermal underwear, a middle layer of fleece, and an outer layer of a waterproof jacket. This keeps you warm and dry. On a hot day, lightweight, breathable clothing is best. A long-sleeved shirt and pants can protect you from the sun and insect bites. A wide-brimmed hat provides shade and keeps the sun off your face. Always carry a rain jacket, even if the forecast looks clear. Weather can change quickly, and it's better to be prepared.

Safety in the wilderness involves being aware of your surroundings, making smart choices, and being prepared. Follow these guidelines, and you'll enjoy your outdoor adventures while staying safe and sound.

HOW TO SIGNAL FOR HELP

Imagine you're out in the wilderness and realize you're lost. The first step in getting help is to signal for it. You can attract attention and let rescuers know where you are in several ways. One of the simplest and most effective methods is using a whistle. A whistle can be heard from a long distance, even if you can't see anyone around. Blow the whistle in three short bursts. This is the international signal of distress. The sound carries well through trees and over hills, making it easy for rescuers to find you.

Another effective way to signal for help is by creating a signal fire. A fire provides warmth and creates smoke that can be seen from far away. To make a signal fire, gather dry wood and kindling. Build a small fire and add green branches or leaves. The green material creates thick, white smoke that stands out against the natural background. Make sure to build your signal fire in an open area where the smoke can rise freely. Always have water or dirt nearby to extinguish the fire once you've been found. We'll discuss fire safety and making fires in Chapter 3: Fire-Making Techniques.

Using mirrors or other reflective surfaces can also be very useful. A small mirror or even a reflective piece of metal can catch the sunlight and flash it over long distances. To use a mirror for signaling, hold it up to catch the sunlight. Tilt the mirror to direct the light toward where you think rescuers might be. Practice this technique at home so you can use it effectively when needed. Flashing a mirror can be seen from miles away, especially if the sky is clear.

Visibility is crucial when signaling for help. You want to make yourself as visible as possible to rescuers. Wearing bright clothing can help you stand out against the natural background. Colors like orange, red, and yellow are easily noticeable. If you have a bright-colored jacket or hat, wear it. Staying in open areas also makes you easier to spot. Avoid hiding under thick trees or in dense bushes. Find a clear spot where you can be seen from above, especially if rescuers use helicopters or planes.

Creating large, noticeable ground signals is another good idea. Use rocks, logs, or brightly colored clothing to spell out SOS or HELP on the ground. These signals can be seen from the air, making it clear that you need assistance. Make the letters as large as possible so they are easily read from a distance. Use contrast to make the signals stand out. For example, white rocks on dark soil or dark logs on light sand. The more noticeable your signal, the faster rescuers can find you.

While waiting for help to arrive, make sure you are safe. First, find or create a shelter to protect yourself from the elements. If you have a tarp or poncho, use it to make a simple shelter. Look for natural shelters like caves or overhangs if you don't have materials with you. We'll talk more about shelters in Chapter 4: Building a Shelter. Conserving energy is also crucial. Stay put once you've signaled for help. Moving around can waste energy and make it harder for rescuers to find you. Drink water regularly to stay hydrated, but ration your supplies if you have a limited amount.

Knowing how to signal for help and what to do while waiting can increase your chances of being found quickly. These skills are simple but very effective. You can practice building shelters and signaling with mirrors at home, preparing you to use them when needed.

STAYING CALM IN EMERGENCY SITUATIONS

Imagine hiking through the woods and suddenly realizing you've lost your way. Your heart races and fear creeps in. In moments like these, staying calm is very important. Staying calm helps you make better decisions and increases your chances of survival. When you panic, your mind gets cloudy, making it hard to think clearly. But, if you stay calm, you can assess the situation, come up with a plan, and act smartly. Reducing panic and fear is the first step to clear thinking and problem-solving.

One way to stay calm is through breathing techniques. Simple breathing exercises can help you manage anxiety. Start by taking deep breaths. Breathe slowly through your nose, hold it for a few seconds, and breathe out through your mouth. This helps slow your heart rate and relaxes your body. Another technique is counting breaths. Breathe in for a count of four, hold for a count of four, and then exhale for a count of four. Visualization can also help. Close your eyes and imagine a peaceful place, like a beach or a meadow. Picture yourself there, feeling calm and safe. These techniques can help you stay focused and relaxed in any situation.

Right after an emergency occurs, it's important to take specific steps to ensure your safety and stability. First, assess the situation. Look around and figure out what happened. Is there an immediate danger? Are there any safe places nearby? Next, check for injuries. See if you or anyone else is hurt. If someone is injured, use your first aid skills to help them. Once you've assessed the situation and checked for injuries, make a plan of action. Decide what steps you need to take next. If you're lost, think about how to signal for help or find your way back. If you're in a dangerous area, move to a safer spot.

Staying calm in emergencies can be tough, but it's possible. In Chapter 10: Real-Life Survival Stories and Challenges, we'll talk about real people who stayed calm in scary situations and found help. These stories show that staying calm can make a big difference. When you stay calm, you can think clearly and make smart decisions. You can use your skills and knowledge to find solutions and stay safe. Remember, emergencies can happen, but staying calm and using the techniques you've learned can help you handle any situation.

CHAPTER THREE
FIRE-MAKING TECHNIQUES

I magine you're camping with your family. The night is cold, and everyone is huddled together. You decide to make a fire to keep everyone warm. You gather some sticks and try to light them, but it doesn't work. You realize you need to know the right way to start a fire. This chapter will teach you how to do that safely and effectively.

FIRE SAFETY BASICS

First and foremost, fire safety is very important. Always have an adult with you when attempting to start a fire. They can help you and make sure everything goes smoothly. Never try to make a fire on your own. Fires can get out of control quickly. Adult supervision ensures that someone can step in if things go wrong. This keeps you and everyone around you safe. Also, never leave a fire unattended. A fire can spread rapidly, even if you think it's small and manageable. Always stay near it until it's completely out. This way, you can control it and prevent any accidents.

Choosing a safe location for your fire is the next step. You need to clear the area of any flammable materials like dry leaves, grass, and sticks. These can catch fire easily and cause the flames to spread. Make sure the ground is bare or covered with rocks. Creating a fire ring with rocks is a good idea. It helps contain the fire and keeps it from spreading. Arrange the rocks in a circle around your fire site. This boundary acts as a barrier and keeps the fire under control. Always choose a site far from trees, bushes, and tents. This reduces the risk of the fire spreading to other areas.

Safety gear is crucial when making a fire. Have a fire blanket or sand nearby to put out the fire if it gets out of control. A fire blanket can smother the flames quickly. Sand can also effectively put out fires by covering the flames and cutting off the oxygen supply. Keep a bucket of water close by. You can use the water to douse the flames if the fire spreads. Knowing how to extinguish a fire safely is as important as knowing how to start one. Always make sure the fire is completely out before you leave the area. Pour water over the fire, stir the ashes, and pour more water until there are no more embers.

Fires can have a significant impact on the environment. It's important to minimize this impact by practicing responsible fire use. Avoid making fires during dry, windy conditions. These conditions can cause the fire to spread quickly and become uncontrollable. Always check the weather forecast before starting a fire. If it's too windy or dry, it's better to skip the fire altogether. When you're done with your fire, restore the site. Scatter the ashes and remove any traces of your fire ring. Leave the area as you found it. This helps protect the environment and ensures that others can enjoy it, too.

Fire Safety Checklist

- Do you have adult supervision or the help of another person?
- Have you picked a safe location with ground that is bare or covered with rocks?
- Do you have a fire blanket, sand, or water to put out the fire?
- Will the weather conditions, like high winds and dry leaves, cause your fire to spread out of control?

Fires are helpful, but they come with responsibility. By following these safety tips, you can enjoy the warmth and comfort of a fire without putting yourself or others at risk. Always remember that safety comes first.

COLLECTING AND PREPARING TINDER AND KINDLING

When you want to start a fire, you need two main things: tinder and kindling. Tinder is a small, easily ignitable material that catches fire quickly. Examples include dry leaves, grass, and pine needles. This is the stuff that makes the initial spark grow into a small flame. On the other hand, kindling consists of small sticks and twigs that catch fire from the tinder. Once the tinder is burning, kindling helps build the fire into something bigger and more stable. Both are necessary for a successful fire. Without tinder, you can't get the fire started. Without kindling, the fire won't grow.

Finding good tinder is critical. Dry leaves are great because they catch fire easily, so look for crisp and crackly leaves. Grass is also good tinder, especially if it's dry and brittle. Pine needles work well, too. They burn quickly and can help get the fire going. In some places, you might find birch bark. This is excellent tinder because it has natural oils that help it burn even when damp. Another good option is cotton balls with petroleum jelly. You can prepare these at home and keep them in a small plastic bag. They catch fire quickly and burn long enough to light the kindling.

Once you have your tinder, you need to find effective kindling. Small sticks and twigs are the best kindling materials. Look for sticks that are about the thickness of a pencil. They should snap easily when you bend them. If they're flexible or damp, they won't burn well. You can also use small branches that you break into shorter pieces. The idea is to have enough kindling to keep the fire going after the tinder catches fire. Collect a good amount of kindling before you start so you don't have to search for more while the fire is burning.

Preparing your tinder and kindling is important. Start by creating a tinder bundle. Gather your tinder materials and form them into a loose ball. This bundle should be small enough to hold in one hand. Make sure it's loose enough for air to flow through, as oxygen helps the fire burn. Next, arrange your kindling in a structure around the tinder bundle. The teepee structure is a good option. Place the tinder bundle in the center and lean the sticks around it like a tent. Another option is the log cabin structure. Lay two sticks parallel on the ground. Place two more sticks on top, perpendicular to the first two. Continue stacking sticks in this pattern to build a small square frame. Place the tinder bundle in the center. Both structures help the fire get enough air to burn well.

Keeping your tinder and kindling dry is crucial. Wet materials won't catch fire easily. If you're gathering materials in the wild, look for dry spots like under trees or rocks. Store your tinder and kindling in a waterproof container. This keeps them dry until you're ready to use them. If you're camping and it starts to rain, use a tarp or plastic bag to cover your fire materials. This prevents them from getting soaked. You can also keep a small stash of tinder in your backpack, protected from moisture.

Gathering, preparing, and storing tinder and kindling directly affect your ability to start and keep fires burning. With knowledge and practice in gathering and readying your tinder and kindling, the once-challenging task of starting a fire becomes another skill you can use to enjoy the wilderness.

USING A MAGNIFYING GLASS TO START A FIRE

Imagine you're out on a sunny day and have a magnifying glass in your backpack. Did you know that you can use it to start a fire? A magnifying glass can focus sunlight onto a small point, making it hot enough to ignite tinder. This process uses the science of focusing sunlight. The curved surface of the magnifying glass gathers sunlight and directs it into a tiny, bright spot. This concentrated light can produce enough heat to start a fire. Not all magnifying glasses are the same, though. Some are better for fire-starting than others. A magnifying glass with a larger lens and high magnification (15-30x) works best. It can focus more sunlight onto the tinder, making it easier to start a fire.

To start a fire with a magnifying glass, you need to follow a few steps. First, find a safe, sunny spot. Lay your tinder on a fire-safe surface. Hold the magnifying glass above the tinder and angle it so the sunlight passes through the lens. You need to adjust the distance between the magnifying glass and the tinder until the light forms a small, bright dot on the tinder. This dot is where the sunlight is most concentrated. Hold the magnifying glass steady and keep the dot focused on one spot. After about 20-30 seconds, you should see the tinder begin to smoke and catch fire.

Using a magnifying glass to start a fire takes patience and practice. It's not always easy to get the angle and distance just right. Practicing on sunny days helps you get better at it. Each time you practice, you'll learn more about how to position the magnifying glass and how long it takes to ignite the tinder. Being patient and persistent is critical. Sometimes, it might take a few tries before you see any smoke. Don't get discouraged. Keep practicing, and you'll get the hang of it.

You must follow some safety precautions while using a magnifying glass to start a fire. Never leave the magnifying glass unattended in sunlight. The focused light can start a fire even when you're not looking. Always keep an eye on it. Avoid looking directly at the focused sunlight through the magnifying glass. The concentrated light can hurt your eyes. And anytime you attempt to start a fire, make sure you have water or sand nearby to put out the fire if needed.

This fire-starting method is useful and fun. It teaches about the power of sunlight and shows how simple tools and natural elements can create something essential for survival.

FIRE MAKING WITH FLINT AND STEEL

Flint and steel have been used to start fires for hundreds of years. Before matches and lighters existed, people used flint and steel to create sparks. This method is reliable and doesn't rely on modern tools. To start a fire with flint and steel, you need three main components: flint, a steel striker, and char cloth. Flint is a type of rock that creates sparks when struck against steel. The steel striker is a piece of metal designed to create sparks when struck against the flint. Char cloth is a piece of cloth that has been charred to make it easily catch sparks. This traditional method is simple but effective and is a great skill to learn.

To start, hold the flint and steel correctly. Place the flint in one hand and the steel striker in the other. Hold the flint steady with the sharp edge facing up. Grip the steel striker firmly. You want to strike the steel against the flint at a sharp angle. This creates a shower of sparks. Position the char cloth close to where the sparks will land. The goal is to catch a spark on the char cloth, which will start to glow. Once the char cloth catches a spark, it will begin to smolder. This is the first step in getting your fire going.

Next, let's look at how to strike the steel to produce sparks. Hold the flint steady and strike the steel down against it firmly. Use a quick, snapping motion to create a burst of sparks. It might take a few tries to get the hang of it. The key is to strike the steel at the right angle and with enough force. As you practice, you'll develop a feel for the right technique. Keep your char cloth positioned to catch the sparks. Once a spark lands on the char cloth, it will glow. This glowing is the sign that you're ready to move to the next step.

Transferring the sparks to tinder is crucial. Carefully pick up the glowing char cloth. Place it in the center of your tinder bundle. Blow gently on the char cloth to help it ignite the tinder. The goal is to create a small flame that you can build into a larger fire. Blowing gently provides the oxygen needed to help the fire grow. Be patient and careful during this step. You want to give enough air without blowing out the glowing char cloth. Once the tinder catches fire, you can add kindling to keep the fire going.

Practicing with flint and steel is important. The more you practice, the better you'll get. Set up regular practice sessions to improve your skills. Try to start a fire with flint and steel in different conditions. Practice on a calm day, but also try when there's a breeze or when it's damp from rain. This helps you understand how to adjust your technique based on the conditions. Developing precision and technique takes time, but you'll become more confident and capable with practice. Don't get discouraged if it doesn't work right away. Keep practicing, and you'll improve.

This method is effective and a great way to connect with the past. People have used flint and steel for centuries; learning this skill helps you understand how they survived. It's a skill that requires patience, practice, and precision. Once you master it, you'll have a reliable way to start a fire in any condition.

Knowing how to make a fire with different methods, like with a magnifying glass or with flint and steel, gives you more options. You're not limited to matches or lighters. This flexibility is helpful in survival situations. Whether you're camping, hiking, or just exploring, these fire-making skills can keep you warm, cook your food, and signal for help. Now that you've learned about fire-making techniques, let's move on to building shelters. Knowing how to stay warm and safe with a fire is essential. But having a good shelter is just as important.

CHAPTER FOUR

BUILDING A SHELTER

I magine you're exploring the woods, and you realize you'll need to spend the night outside. You need a shelter to stay warm and safe. If you don't have a tent, this chapter will teach you skills for building a shelter. First, you need to choose the right location. The spot you pick can make a big difference. A good location protects you from wind and rain. It also keeps you close to resources like water and firewood. A bad location can put you in danger from falling branches, flooding, insects, or animals.

PICKING YOUR SHELTER SITE

Choosing a good location for your shelter begins by looking for flat and dry ground. Starting with a flat surface makes the building process easier and makes sleeping in your shelter more comfortable. Check the ground for stability once you find a flat, dry area. Make sure it's free of rocks and roots. Rocks can be uncomfortable to sleep on, and roots can make the ground uneven. Steer clear of low-lying areas where water is likely to gather. These areas are prone to flooding, especially during heavy rain, which can soak your shelter and make it soggy. Any gear or supplies you have in your shelter when it floods will get wet or, even worse, completely ruined. Seek out natural barriers against the wind, such as large boulders or clusters of dense foliage. These natural formations can serve as effective windbreaks, shielding your shelter from harsh, chilling winds. By strategically placing your shelter behind these barriers, you can make your shelter more cozy by reducing the wind's impact on your sleeping area.

When you're looking for a spot, consider the environment. Try to use existing clearings to minimize your environmental impact. But, more importantly, you don't have to clear a lot of vegetation to save energy for other survival tasks. Keep a safe distance from insect nests and avoid areas with visible animal trails. Encountering insects can lead to a restless night filled with discomfort and potential bites or stings.

Similarly, setting up camp too close to an animal trail may disturb local wildlife, as these paths are often routes for animals to access water, food, or shelter. Respecting their space protects you from unexpected wildlife encounters but also prevents you from disrupting the natural habits and movements of the area's inhabitants. Always follow the "Leave No Trace" principles. This means leaving the area as you found it. Don't leave behind any trash or damage.

Shelter Site Checklist

- Is the ground flat and dry?
- Are you away from low areas where water might collect?
- Is the ground free of rocks and roots?
- Are you near natural windbreaks like large rocks or dense trees?
- Are you using existing clearings?
- Are you away from insect nests and animal trails?

Use this checklist to help you find the perfect spot for your shelter. Once you have a good location, you can start building. Your shelter will protect you from the elements and help you get a good night's rest. These skills make you feel more confident and ready for any adventure.

BUILDING A LEAN-TO SHELTER

A lean-to shelter is one of the simplest and quickest shelters you can build. It's great for protecting yourself from wind and rain and works well in many different environments. You don't need a lot of materials to build it, either, which makes it perfect for survival situations. You can set it up quickly, which is good if you need shelter quickly.

To build a lean-to, you'll need a long, sturdy branch for the primary support. This branch will act as the backbone of your shelter. You'll also need smaller branches to form the frame. These branches should be strong enough to hold up leaves, grass, or bark for insulation. Finally, you'll need materials to cover the frame. Leaves, grass, and bark work well. They help keep the shelter warm and dry. If you have a tarp, that can make your shelter even better.

First, find a strong, horizontal support. This could be a fallen tree or a large rock. The support should be sturdy enough to hold the weight of the branches and covering materials. Once you have your support, start leaning the smaller branches against it. Place the thicker ends of the branches on the ground and the thinner end against the support. Arrange the branches close together to form a solid frame. The frame should look like a slanted wall leaning against the support.

Next, cover the frame with insulating materials. Start by layering leaves, grass, or bark over the branches. You want to cover the entire frame to keep the wind and rain out. The more layers you add, the better the insulation. If you have a tarp, drape it over the frame for extra protection. Make sure the tarp is secure and won't blow away. Use rocks or branches to hold it in place if needed.

Securing the structure is important. Use additional branches and materials to strengthen the shelter. You can weave smaller branches through the frame to make it more stable. This helps keep the shelter intact, even in strong wind. Make sure everything is tightly packed. There should be no gaps for wind or rain to get through.

Add a layer of leaves or pine boughs on the ground to make your lean-to more comfortable. This creates a soft floor and adds extra insulation. You can also create a small fire reflector wall nearby. Use rocks or logs to build a low wall in front of the shelter. This reflects heat from your fire into the shelter, keeping you warmer. Make sure the opening of the lean-to faces away from the wind. This helps keep the wind out and the warmth in.

Building a lean-to-shelter is a valuable skill. It's quick to set up, provides good protection, and works in many different settings. With practice, you can build a lean-to that keeps you safe and comfortable in the wilderness.

CONSTRUCTING A DEBRIS HUT

A debris hut is one of the best shelters you can build when it's cold outside. It keeps you warm by providing excellent insulation. This shelter uses natural materials like leaves, grass, and sticks. These materials are easy to find, making the debris hut a great option in many situations. Besides keeping you warm, a debris hut also provides good camouflage. This means it blends in with the surroundings, making it harder for animals to see you. It can keep you safe and snug through the night if built well.

To build a debris hut, you need a few critical materials. First, you need a sturdy branch for the ridge pole. This branch will act as the primary support for your shelter. It should be strong enough to hold up the rest of the structure. Next, gather smaller branches to create the frame. These branches should be sturdy but flexible enough to weave together. Finally, you'll need lots of leaves, grass, and other debris for insulation. The more debris you have, the warmer your shelter will be.

Start by placing the ridge pole between two supports. Look for forked trees or large rocks to hold the ends of the ridge pole. The ridge pole should be about chest height. This gives you enough space inside the shelter. Once the ridge pole is in place, lean the smaller branches against it to create a frame. These branches should form a triangular shape with the ground. Make sure they are close together to make a solid structure.

Next, pile leaves and other debris on the frame. Start at the bottom and work your way up. You want a thick insulation layer to keep the wind and cold out. Use as much debris as you can find. The thicker the layer, the warmer the shelter. Make sure the debris covers the entire frame. You don't want any gaps where wind can get through. Pile leaves, grass, and small branches until the whole frame is covered.

The next step is to create an entrance. Leave a small opening at one end of the shelter. This is where you'll crawl in and out. Make sure the entrance is just big enough for you to fit through. You want to keep it small to keep the warmth inside. Once the entrance is in place, insulate it with additional debris. You can use more leaves and grass to cover the entrance when you're inside. This helps keep the warmth in and the cold out.

To improve your debris hut, you can add extra layers of debris for better insulation. Keep piling leaves and grass until the walls are thick and sturdy. This makes the shelter warmer and more comfortable. Creating a raised bed inside the hut is another good idea. Use small branches and leaves to make a bed off the ground. This helps keep you warmer by insulating you from the cold ground. Finally, make sure the structure is waterproof by adding more debris on top. This helps keep rain and snow out, making your shelter more durable.

Building a debris hut takes time and effort, but it's worth it. It's one of the best shelters for cold weather. It uses natural materials that are easy to find. It provides excellent insulation and good protection from wildlife. With practice, you can build a debris hut that keeps you warm and safe in the wilderness.

CREATING A TARP SHELTER

Imagine you're on a hike, and it starts raining. You need quick shelter to stay dry. A tarp shelter is perfect for this situation. It's fast and easy to set up. It's also lightweight and portable, making it great for carrying in your backpack. Plus, a tarp shelter works in various weather conditions. Whether it's rain, wind, or even a bit of snow, a tarp can help keep you protected.

To build a tarp shelter, you'll need a few items. First, you need a tarp or a large piece of plastic sheeting, which will be your primary cover. You'll also need a paracord or strong rope to tie and secure the tarp. Tent stakes or sturdy sticks are necessary to hold the tarp in place. These items are easy to carry and only take up a little space in your pack.

Start by choosing a good site and clearing the ground. Find a spot that's flat and free of sharp objects like rocks and sticks. This makes your shelter more comfortable to sleep in. Next, tie your strong rope between two trees or supports. The cord should be tight and about waist height. This will be the ridge line for your tarp. Drape the tarp over the ridge line to form a roof. Make sure the tarp is centered and covers both sides evenly.

Secure the corners of the tarp with stakes or sticks. Push the stakes or sticks into the ground at an angle to keep the tarp tight. This helps prevent the tarp from flapping in the wind. You can use rocks or heavy logs to hold down the corners if you don't have stakes. Adjust the tarp as needed to make sure it's tight and stable.

If you have more tarps or plastic sheets in your pack, you can use them to improve your tarp shelter. Consider making a ground-sheet with an extra tarp or piece of plastic. Staying dry is crucial for outdoor survival, especially in cold conditions. A groundsheet can be a barrier between you and the ground, preventing moisture from dampening your clothes and sleeping gear and adding an essential insulation layer. This insulation is critical to retaining your body heat, protecting you from the cold ground that can significantly lower your body temperature.

Adjusting the tarp's height and angle can also make a big differ-ence. You can lower one side of the tarp to create a barrier that shields you from gusty winds and driving rain, keeping the inside of your shelter dry and warm. After lowering one side of the tarp, consider raising the opposite side to open up space for air to circu-late. Raising one side of the tarp could improve ventilation and make your shelter feel less cramped. This balance between protec-tion and airflow is vital to building an effective shelter.

Building a tarp shelter is a valuable skill. It's quick, easy, and works in many different conditions. You can create a shelter that keeps you dry and warm with just a few items. Practice setting up a tarp shelter at home so you're ready when you need it. The more you practice, the faster and better you'll get.

Survival skills like building shelters are important. They help you stay safe and comfortable in the wilderness. Whether you're on a hike, camping, or in an emergency, knowing how to create a shelter makes a big difference. Next, we'll explore other survival skills that can help you even more.

CHAPTER FIVE
FINDING AND PURIFYING WATER

I magine you've been hiking all day with your friends. The sun is hot, and your water bottle is empty. You're thirsty, and you know you need to find water soon. Water is one of the most important things you need to survive. Your body depends on it to keep everything working. Without enough water, you can get sick very quickly. Knowing how to find and purify water can make a big difference.

IDENTIFYING NATURAL WATER SOURCES

Finding water is crucial for survival. Your body needs water for hydration and to keep bodily functions working smoothly. Water helps your body regulate temperature, digest food, and remove waste. When you don't get enough water, you can become dehydrated. Dehydration makes your mouth dry, gives you headaches, and makes you feel dizzy. Severe dehydration can make you very weak and even cause serious health problems. That's why it's important to find water as soon as possible if you run out.

Knowing how to locate water in the wild can save your life. One way to find water is by following animal tracks. Animals need water just like you do, so their tracks often lead to water sources. Look for paths worn down by animals. These paths often lead to streams or ponds. Another clue is green vegetation. Plants need water to grow, so areas with many green plants usually have water nearby. Listen for the sound of running water. The sound of a stream or river can guide you to a water source, even if you can't see it yet.

Different types of water sources have their pros and cons. Streams and rivers are good sources of flowing water. Flowing water is less likely to be stagnant and can be safer to drink after purification. However, rivers and streams can also carry pollutants from upstream, so always purify the water before drinking. Lakes and ponds can be good sources, too, but the water might be stagnant. Stagnant water can have bacteria and other harmful organisms, so it's important to purify it. Rainwater collection is another option. You can use a tarp or leaves to collect rainwater. Rainwater is usually clean, but purifying it is still a good idea. Natural springs are one of the best sources. Springs bring water from underground, which is often cleaner. If you find a spring, drinking after purification is usually safe.

When choosing a water source, it's important to minimize contamination risks. Avoid stagnant water, which can be a breeding ground for bacteria. Always look for signs of pollution. If the water has an unusual color, smell, or floating debris, it might be contaminated. It's safer to find another source.

Water Source Checklist

- Look for animal tracks leading to water.
- Check for green vegetation that indicates water nearby.

- Listen for the sound of running water.
- Choose flowing water from streams and rivers.
- Collect rainwater using tarps or leaves.
- Find natural springs if possible.
- Avoid stagnant water.
- Check for signs of pollution.

Finding water in the wild is a vital skill. It keeps you hydrated and healthy. Learning how to locate and choose safe water sources can help you stay safe in any situation.

SAFE WATER COLLECTION TECHNIQUES

When you're out in the wild, collecting water safely is critical. The first step is to use a clean container or bottle that is free of dirt and debris.

Having the right tools can make water collection easier. Water bottles and canteens are great for storing and carrying water. They're lightweight and easy to pack. Portable water filters are handy for outdoor adventurers. These compact, easy-to-use devices can effectively remove dirt, sediment, and harmful microorganisms directly from the water source. Ideal for filling up from streams, rivers, or lakes, portable water filters offer a quick and efficient way to access clean drinking water. A lightweight tarp is handy for catching rain. You can place the tarp at an angle so the water runs off into your container. This method is simple and effective, especially during a good rain. If you have multiple tarps, you can set them up in the rain to collect more water than with just one tarp. If you don't have any tarps, look for large leaves that you can use to collect rain.

Another way to collect water is by scooping it from a stream. But be careful not to disturb the bottom. Stirring up mud can make the water dirty and hard to purify. Always scoop water from the surface where it's clearer. To avoid contaminants when collecting water, use a cloth or bandana to filter out debris. Place the fabric over your container and pour the water through it. Filtering the water through cloth will prevent some particles or sediment in the water from entering your container.

When collecting water from a stream, always make sure you collect water upstream from any potential sources of contamination. This means positioning yourself away from areas where animals might frequent or where runoff from rain could introduce pollutants into the water. Choosing a collection point closer to the stream's origin makes you more likely to access cleaner, less contaminated water. Steer clear of areas where water appears green or murky due to algae. Even after being purified, water with algae might still pose health risks due to possible toxins that can't be eliminated through simple purification methods. Instead, look for clear running water that will be safer and healthier to drink.

BOILING WATER FOR PURIFICATION

When you're out in the wild and find water, it's important to make sure it's safe to drink. Untreated water can have harmful pathogens like bacteria, viruses, and parasites. These tiny organisms can make you very sick. Drinking contaminated water can lead to stomach pains, diarrhea, and even more severe health problems. That's why purifying water is so important. By boiling water, you can kill most of these harmful organisms. This makes the water safe to drink and helps keep you healthy and strong.

To purify water by boiling, you'll need a heat-resistant container. This could be a metal pot or a heat-proof bottle. First, collect the water in your container. Make sure to use clean water from the best source available. Once you have your water, it's time to build a fire. We discussed fire safety and making fires in Chapter 3: Fire-Making Techniques. Place the container over the fire. You can do this by setting it on a rock or using a makeshift tripod made from sticks. Watch the water closely. You need to bring it to a rolling boil. This means the water should be bubbling vigorously. Keep it boiling for at least one minute. This ensures that harmful organisms are killed. If you're at a high altitude, boil the water for three minutes. After boiling, let the water cool naturally before drinking.

Boiling water has many benefits. It's very effective at killing most pathogens. This makes it one of the safest methods to purify water. However, boiling water also has some limitations. You need a heat source, like a fire, and a suitable container. This can be a challenge if you don't have the right supplies. Boiling water is also time-consuming. It takes time to gather materials, build a fire, and wait for the water to boil and cool. Despite these limitations, boiling water is a reliable method to ensure clean drinking water.

Before boiling, it's a good idea to pre-filter the water. If you don't have a portable water filter, pour the water through a cloth or bandana to remove particles and sediment. This makes the boiling process more effective. You can use smaller containers to boil water faster. When you heat a smaller amount of water, it reaches the boiling point quicker than a larger volume, saving you time. Smaller amounts of water cool off faster than larger amounts, too. It's also a good idea to cover the water container while you're boiling the water. Use a lid or a piece of aluminum foil to cover the water container to reduce heat loss and speed up the boiling process by trapping heat inside.

Knowing how to boil water for purification is a valuable skill. It can help you stay safe and healthy in the wild. By following these steps, you can make sure the water you drink is clean and safe. This keeps you hydrated and ready for your next adventure.

USING WATER PURIFICATION TABLETS

Water purification tablets can make water safe to drink by using chemicals like iodine or chlorine. They work by neutralizing harmful pathogens in the water, killing bacteria, viruses, and other germs that can make you sick. The tablets are easy to carry and use, making them a great tool for any outdoor adventure.

Using water purification tablets is simple if you follow the instructions. First, read the instructions on the tablet packaging carefully. Each brand may have slightly different directions. Usually, you'll need to add one or two tablets to a specific amount of water. Make sure you use the right number of tablets for the amount of water you have. Next, drop the tablets into your water bottle or container. Shake or stir the water to help the tablets dissolve completely. This ensures the chemicals mix well with the water. After that, wait for the required amount of time. This is usually about 30 minutes, but it can vary. Waiting gives the chemicals time to kill any harmful organisms in the water.

Water purification tablets have many advantages. They are lightweight and portable, so you can easily carry them in your backpack. This makes them perfect for long hikes or camping trips. The tablets are also easy to use with minimal equipment. You don't need a fire, pot, or special tools—just a container to hold the water. However, there are some drawbacks. The chemicals can change the taste of the water. Some people find the taste of iodine or chlorine unpleasant. Also, the tablets are not effective against certain chemicals or heavy metals that might be in the water. They only kill germs, so you'll need another purification method if the water is polluted with chemicals.

To make sure the tablets work effectively, use clear water whenever possible. The cleaner the water, the better the tablets will work. If the water is dirty or cloudy, pre-filter it through a cloth or bandana to remove particles and sediment. This helps the tablets do their job more efficiently. Store the tablets in a cool, dry place to maintain their potency. Heat and moisture can reduce their effectiveness. Combining tablets with other methods can also improve safety. For example, you can boil the water first and then use the tablets to kill germs. This ensures the water is as clean as possible. By knowing how to use these tablets, you can make sure you have clean water to drink, even if you don't have other purification tools with you.

Water is essential for your body to function correctly. Having the skills to find and purify water can keep you safe and healthy in any outdoor adventure. Whether hiking, camping, or exploring, knowing how to purify water ensures you're prepared for any situation. Next, we'll explore other important survival skills that can help you thrive in the wilderness.

MAKE A DIFFERENCE WITH YOUR REVIEW
SHARE THE ADVENTURE WITH OTHERS

"No act of kindness, no matter how small, is ever wasted."

AESOP

Helping others is like shining a light in the dark. Let's make a big difference together!

Would you like to help another kid who's excited to learn outdoor survival skills but doesn't know where to start?

My mission is to make learning survival skills easy and fun for kids like you, so you can explore nature with confidence.

But I need your help to reach more young adventurers.

Most people choose books by reading reviews. So, I'm asking you to share your thoughts about **Secrets of Outdoor Survival Skills for Kids Revealed**.

It costs nothing and takes less than a minute, but your review could light the way for...

- ...one more kid to feel brave in the wilderness.
- ...one more family to enjoy adventures together.
- ...one more child to discover the wonders of nature.
- ...one more young explorer to learn how to stay safe outdoors.

To help make a difference, please scan the QR code below and leave a review:

Leave a Review

If you love helping others, you're a true hero. Thank you from the bottom of my heart!

- **Brent Marshall**

CHAPTER SIX
FORAGING AND IDENTIFYING EDIBLE PLANTS

I magine you're walking through a meadow on a warm summer day. You see all kinds of plants and flowers around you. Some of these plants could be tasty and nutritious. Foraging is the practice of identifying and collecting plants that grow wild in nature. It's like a treasure hunt where the prize is delicious and healthy food. But before you start picking and eating, knowing which plants are safe is crucial. This chapter will teach you how to forage safely and responsibly.

BASIC RULES OF FORAGING

Before you start foraging, you must know about the plants around you. Understanding plant identification is very important. Some plants are safe to eat, while others can be harmful. Knowing the local flora, or the types of plants that grow in your area, helps you identify edible plants correctly. This knowledge protects you from eating something that could make you sick. Researching and educating yourself regularly is vital. Use books, field guides, or apps to learn about different plants. The more you know, the safer and more successful your foraging will be.

One helpful method for identifying plants is the "3-Part Rule." This rule helps ensure a plant is safe to eat by examining three main parts: the leaves, the flowers, and the fruits or seeds. Start by examining the leaves. Look at their shape, size, and color. Some plants have unique leaves that make them easy to identify. Next, check the flowers. Flowers can be very distinctive, with specific colors and patterns. Finally, observe the fruits or seeds. These can also have unique features that help you identify the plant. You can make a more accurate identification by looking at these three parts.

Always remember the "When in Doubt, Leave it Out" principle. If you're not 100% sure that a plant is safe to eat, don't eat it. Being cautious and conservative keeps you safe. It's better to miss out on a potentially tasty plant than to risk getting sick. If you're unsure, consult a field guide or an expert. Never consume a plant based on partial identification. Eating something without being sure can lead to serious health problems. Safety should always come first.

Foraging responsibly is important for protecting plant populations and their habitats. Take only what you need. This ensures that there are enough plants left for wildlife and future growth. Overharvesting can damage the environment and make it harder for plants to regrow. Avoid taking too much from any one area. Spread out your foraging to different locations to minimize impact. This helps keep the ecosystem balanced and healthy.

Here are some tips for sustainable foraging:

- Take only what you need, leaving enough for wildlife.
- Avoid overharvesting in any one area.
- Be mindful of endangered or rare plants and leave them alone.
- Use a field guide to identify plants accurately.

Foraging can be a fun and rewarding activity. It helps you connect with nature and learn about the plants around you. By following these basic rules, you can forage safely and responsibly. Always remember that knowledge is your best tool. The more you know about plants, the better your foraging experience will be.

IDENTIFYING COMMON EDIBLE PLANTS

When you're out exploring nature, you'll find many plants that are safe to eat, delicious, and nutritious. Knowing how to identify these plants can turn your hike into a fun and tasty adventure. Let's look at some common edible plants that you can find in various regions.

Dandelions are one of the easiest plants to identify. They have bright yellow flowers that look like little suns. Their leaves are toothed, which means they have edges that look like tiny teeth. Dandelions grow just about everywhere, from fields to sidewalks. Dandelions are not only widespread but can serve a nutritious purpose. They are packed with vitamins A, C, and K, which are crucial in maintaining your health. For instance, vitamin A is used by your body for good vision, vitamin C is used by your body to boost your immune system, and vitamin K is used by your body to strengthen your bones and heal wounds. When foraging for dandelions, pick the leaves before the flowers bloom. The younger leaves are less bitter and taste better than the older leaves.

Clover is another common plant that's easy to find. Clover is easy to spot with its distinctive three-leaf clusters and small, delicate flowers. Rich in protein and packed with essential minerals such as calcium, magnesium, and potassium, clover is an excellent plant to eat to keep you going. These nutrients are vital for maintaining strong bones, supporting nerve and muscle function, and helping to regulate fluid balance in the body. Clover flowers have a mild, sweet flavor. Always wash the flowers thoroughly before eating them.

Strawberries are a sweet treat you can find in the wild. Wild strawberries have small red berries and serrated leaves. The berries are much smaller than the ones you buy in the store, but they pack a lot of flavor. Wild strawberries are packed with antioxidants, which help protect your body from harmful substances. The wild strawberries you want to pick will have a deep red color, meaning they are ripe and at their peak of sweetness. Use a gentle touch to avoid bruising them. After picking, wash the strawberries to remove any dirt, insects, or natural debris before consuming.

Chickweed is not a well-known plant, but it grows in many environments. You can identify chickweed by its tiny, star-shaped white blossoms and green, smooth leaves. Chickweed typically grows in cooler, shaded spots and is rich in vitamin C, iron, and magnesium. We already talked about the benefits of vitamin C. Still, iron and magnesium are used by your body for many internal processes like replenishing red blood cells and regulating your nervous system. Chickweed's leaves have a slightly nutty flavor. Focus on collecting the younger, greener leaves for the most flavor.

When you're hunting for edible plants, it's important to gather them properly. Whenever possible, wash the plants before eating them. Wild strawberries should be eaten soon after picking them. Dandelions, clover, and chickweed leaves can be eaten raw or cooked. Foraging for edible plants is a fun and rewarding activity. It helps you connect with nature and learn more about the plants around you. By knowing how to identify and harvest these common edible plants, you can enjoy a variety of tasty and nutritious foods right from the wild.

AVOIDING POISONOUS PLANTS

When exploring and foraging, knowing which plants to avoid is important. Some plants look harmless but can be very dangerous. Recognizing common poisonous plants is a crucial skill for foraging and can keep you safe. Here are some tips to help you identify some common poisonous plants.

The first poisonous plant you should be familiar with is Poison Ivy. This plant has three-leaf clusters and shiny leaves; the middle leaf is usually longer than the other two. The leaves turn red in the fall, making them easier to spot. The saying "Leaves of three, let it be" can help you remember. Poison Ivy often grows as a vine or low shrub. Touching it can cause itchy skin rashes and blisters. The rash can spread if you touch the oil and then touch other parts of your body.

Poison Oak is similar to Poison Ivy but has leaves that look like oak leaves. The leaves come in threes and can be shiny or dull, and they often change colors with the seasons. Like Poison Ivy, poison oak causes skin rashes and irritation. It is found mostly in the western United States. If you see a plant with three leaves that look like oak leaves, stay away from it.

Poison Hemlock is another plant you need to watch out for. It's a tall plant with white umbrella-shaped flowers. Poison Hemlock can grow up to ten feet high. The stem has purple spots, which are a vital feature for identification. Poison Hemlock is highly toxic. Even a small amount can cause serious health issues. If you accidentally eat it, you could experience nausea, vomiting, and respiratory problems. In severe cases, it can lead to hospitalization. Always avoid tall plants with white flowers and purple-spotted stems.

Deadly Nightshade is a plant you definitely want to avoid. It has oval-shaped leaves and bell-shaped purple flowers. The berries are shiny and black when ripe. The berries might look like blackberries, but they are very dangerous. Eating even a few berries can cause serious symptoms like hallucinations, confusion, and severe stomach pain. Deadly Nightshade can be found in many places, including forests and gardens. Always avoid plants with dark, shiny berries and bell-shaped flowers.

Knowing the dangers of poisonous plants helps you understand why it's important to avoid them. Touching or eating these plants can cause skin rashes, nausea, and respiratory issues. The symptoms can range from mild to severe. In some cases, exposure can lead to hospitalization. Skin rashes and irritation are the most common symptoms. They can be very itchy and uncomfortable. Nausea and vomiting can make you feel very sick. Respiratory issues are more serious and can make it hard to breathe. Severe toxicity can cause confusion and hallucinations and even be life-threatening.

If you accidentally touch or ingest a poisonous plant, acting quickly is important. The first step is to wash the affected area with water. This helps remove any plant oils that can cause skin irritation. If you start to feel sick, seek medical help immediately. Tell an adult what happened so they can help you get the care you need. Identifying and reporting the plant can help doctors treat your symptoms more effectively. They might ask you to describe the plant or even bring a piece of it for identification.

Recognizing and avoiding these plants can keep you safe while exploring and foraging. Knowing what to do if you come into contact with them can help you act quickly and get the care you need. Awareness of your surroundings and the plants you encounter is crucial for a safe and enjoyable outdoor adventure.

SAFE FORAGING PRACTICES

When you're out foraging, always have an adult with you. This is very important for your safety, as adults have more experience and knowledge about plants. They can teach you which are safe to eat and which to avoid. Having an adult means you have immediate help if something goes wrong. If you get a cut or feel sick, an adult can take care of you right away. This makes your foraging trips safer and more enjoyable. You also get to learn hands-on, which is the best way to understand and remember what you've learned. Watching and helping an adult forage gives you practical experience that you can use in the future.

Using a field guide is a big help when you're trying to identify plants. A field guide is a book that has pictures and descriptions of plants. It helps you identify plants by comparing their features with the illustrations in the guide. Start by looking at the plant's leaves, flowers, and fruits. Compare these features with the pictures in the guide. Read the descriptions and notes carefully. They provide important details that help you make a positive identification. Always bring the field guide with you on foraging trips. It's a useful tool that helps you learn more about the plants you find.

Keeping clean is also very important when you're foraging. You don't want to get sick from dirt or germs on your hands or plants. Always wash your hands before eating. Use water or hand sanitizer to get rid of any dirt and germs. Clean the plants you collect thoroughly. Rinse them in clean water to remove dirt and bugs. Using clean containers for gathering is also important. Dirty containers can contaminate the plants you've collected. Make sure your containers are clean before you start foraging.

Once you've collected your plants, you need to store and preserve them properly to keep them fresh and safe to eat. Store the plants in cool, dry places. This helps keep them fresh and prevents them from spoiling. Use containers to protect the plants from pests. Bugs and animals can ruin your hard-earned foraged plants. Containers keep them safe and fresh. For long-term preservation, you can dry or freeze the plants. Drying is a good way to preserve leaves and herbs. Hang them in a dry, airy place until they're completely dry. Then, store them in airtight containers.

Foraging is a fun and rewarding activity that helps you learn more about the plants around you. By following these safe foraging practices, you can enjoy your foraging trips safely and responsibly. Always forage with an adult, use a field guide, keep clean, and store your plants properly. These practices help you stay safe and make the most of your foraging adventures.

CHAPTER SEVEN

NAVIGATIONAL SKILLS

I magine you're on a hike with your friends. You take a turn and suddenly realize you're not sure which way to go. Your phone's battery is dead, and you don't have a GPS. What do you do? Knowing how to read a map can help you find your way. It's like having a secret tool that guides you back to safety. Let's explore how you can master this skill and never feel lost again.

READING A MAP: BASICS AND BEYOND

Maps come in different types, each serving a unique purpose. Understanding these types helps you choose the right map for your adventure. Topographic maps show the terrain and elevation of an area. They help you understand the shape of the land, like hills and valleys. These maps are great for hiking and exploring. Road maps detail highways and major routes. They help you navigate cities and long car trips. These maps show roads, exits, and important landmarks. Trail maps highlight hiking paths and landmarks in parks or forests. They guide you along trails and show points of interest like campsites and water sources.

Reading a map means understanding its symbols and legends. Contour lines on a topographic map indicate elevation changes. The closer the lines, the steeper the terrain. Wide spaces between lines mean a gentle slope. Knowing how to read these lines helps you understand the land's shape. Symbols for water bodies, trails, and campsites are also important. Blue lines or shapes usually represent rivers and lakes. Dotted lines often indicate trails. Little tent symbols show where campsites are. The map legend explains all these symbols. It's like a key that helps you decode the map. Always check the legend to understand what each symbol means.

Orienting a map with the landscape is crucial for accurate navigation. Start by matching map features with real-world landmarks. Look for hills, rivers, or buildings on the map and find them in your surroundings. This helps you know where you are on the map. Using a compass makes this even easier. Place the compass on the map with the direction of travel arrow pointing to the top. Rotate the map and compass together until the magnetic needle aligns with the north-south lines on the map. This means your map is now oriented correctly.

Practice Exercise: Mapping Out a Simple Route

Take a trail map of a local park. Choose a starting point and a destination. Use a pencil to draw a line connecting the two points. Look for landmarks along the way, like streams or rocks. Practice identifying these landmarks on your hike. This helps you understand how to use the map in real life.

Understanding maps and how to use them can give you a sense of independence. You'll feel more confident exploring new places. It's like having a treasure map that helps you uncover the world around you.

USING A COMPASS

Imagine you are in a forest with tall trees all around. You want to find your way back to camp, but the trees look the same in every direction. A compass can help you find the right path. Understanding the parts of a compass is the first step. The baseplate is the flat surface of the compass. It has straight edges that help you take bearings. The magnetic needle points to magnetic North. This needle is usually red or white. The rotating bezel, also called the azimuth ring, is used to set bearings. It has 360-degree markings that help you find directions.

To use a compass and take a bearing, start by holding the compass flat and steady in your hand. Make sure the baseplate is level. Next, turn your body until the magnetic needle lines up with the orienting arrow on the bezel. The orienting arrow is usually a small arrow inside the bezel. Now, look at the numbers on the bezel. The number that lines up with the index line is your bearing. This number tells you the direction you need to go. For example, if your bearing is 90 degrees, you need to walk East.

Once you have your bearing, it's time to follow it. Keep the compass level and the needle aligned with the orienting arrow. Start walking in the direction of your bearing. Make sure to check the compass regularly to stay on course. Walk in a straight line and avoid obstacles like trees or rocks. If you need to go around an obstacle, use landmarks to help you stay on track. For example, pick a tree in the distance and walk towards it. Once you reach the tree, take another bearing to continue in the right direction.

Sometimes, you might have problems with your compass. Magnetic interference from metal objects can cause problems. Avoid using your compass near metal items like pocket knives, zippers, or even large rocks with iron. These can affect the magnetic needle and give you a wrong reading. Make sure to move away from any metal objects before taking a bearing. Weather conditions can also impact the accuracy of your compass. In cold weather, the magnetic needle might move more slowly. Hold the compass close to your body to keep it warm. In stormy weather, strong winds can make it hard to keep the compass level. Find a sheltered spot to take your bearings.

Using a compass might seem tricky at first, but with practice, it becomes easier. By understanding the parts of a compass and learning how to take and follow bearings, you can navigate safely through the wilderness. Practice these skills in a familiar area before trying them in more challenging locations. This way, you'll feel more confident and prepared when you need to find your way.

NAVIGATING USING THE SUN AND STARS

Imagine you are outside on a bright day and need to find your way. The sun can be a helpful guide. The sun rises in the East and sets in the West. Knowing this helps you find directions. In the morning, if you face the rising sun, East is in front of you, West is behind you, North is to your left, and South is to your right. In the afternoon, when the sun is setting, the directions switch. Facing the setting sun means West is in front of you, East is behind you, North is to your right, and South is to your left. This basic understanding of the sun's movement can help you stay oriented.

Using a shadow stick is another way to find directions with the sun. Find a straight stick and push it into the ground so it stands upright. Mark the stick's tip of the shadow with a small rock or another stick. Wait about 15 minutes, then mark the tip of the shadow again. Draw a line between the two marks. This line runs from East to West. The first mark is west, and the second mark is east. Stand with the first mark on your left and the second mark on your right. Now, you are facing north. This simple method helps you find the cardinal directions even without a compass.

If you have an analog watch, you can use it to find North. Hold the watch flat with the hour hand pointing at the sun. Imagine a line running from the center of the watch between the hour hand and the 12 o'clock mark. This line points south. North is in the opposite direction. This trick works best when the sun is high in the sky, so it might be less accurate early in the morning or late in the afternoon. However, it's a useful backup method when you need it.

At night, the stars can help you find your way. The North Star, or Polaris, is crucial for navigation in the Northern Hemisphere. It always points north. To find the North Star, look for the Big Dipper constellation. The Big Dipper looks like a large spoon or ladle. Find the two stars at the edge of the Big Dipper's "bowl." Draw an imaginary line through these stars and extend it outward. The first bright star you see along this line is the North Star. Once you find the North Star, you know which way is North.

Other constellations can also help you navigate. The Big Dipper is part of a larger constellation called Ursa Major, the Great Bear. Just below the North Star is the Little Dipper, which is part of Ursa Minor, the Little Bear. Learning to recognize these constellations helps you find your way at night. The constellations look the same every night, making them reliable guides. Practice finding these constellations on clear nights to become more familiar with them.

If you are in the Southern Hemisphere, you can use the Southern Cross constellation to help you find your way. The Southern Cross is made up of four bright stars and one dim star, but the fifth dim star is not part of the cross shape. Draw imaginary lines between the four bright stars to make a cross. Next, draw an imaginary line from the end of the longer line all the way down to the horizon. The spot where your imaginary line meets the horizon is south.

Practical Exercise: Navigating with a Shadow Stick

Find a sunny spot and push a stick into the ground. Mark the tip of its shadow with a small rock. Wait 15 minutes and mark the shadow's tip again. Draw a line between the two marks. Stand with the first mark on your left and the second on your right. You are now facing north. Practice this until you can do it quickly and accurately.

Navigating with the sun and stars is a valuable skill. It helps you stay oriented when other tools aren't available. Practice these methods during your outdoor adventures to become more confident. When you understand how to use the sun and stars, you'll always have a way to find your direction.

CREATING A SIMPLE TRAIL MARKER SYSTEM

Imagine you're exploring a dense forest with your friends. The trees look the same, and the paths twist and turn. Trail markers can help you find your way back. They act like breadcrumbs, guiding you through the woods. Marking trails helps you retrace your steps and avoid getting lost. It also lets you communicate directions to others in your group. If someone gets separated, they can follow the markers to find their way back. This makes exploring safer and more fun.

Creating natural markers is easy and doesn't require special tools. One way is to stack rocks to form cairns. A cairn is a small pile of rocks that stands out against the natural landscape. Find a few flat stones and stack them on top of each other. Make sure they are stable and won't fall over easily. Another method is to arrange sticks in patterns on the ground. You can create arrows pointing in the direction you need to go. Look for straight sticks and lay them out in a clear arrow shape. This helps others understand which way to go. Brightly colored ribbons or fabric strips are also useful. Tie them to branches at eye level. The bright colors are easy to spot, even from a distance.

When making trail markers, it's important to leave no trace. This means you should avoid damaging plants and trees. Don't break branches or pull up plants to make your markers. Instead, use materials that are already on the ground. Ensure your markers are easily removable. When you're done with your hike, remove any markers you made. This keeps the environment clean and natural for others to enjoy. It's a good habit that protects nature and shows respect for the outdoors.

Practice Exercise: Setting Up a Trail

Find a safe area in a local park or your backyard. Set up a short trail using natural markers. Use rocks to create cairns and sticks to form arrows. You can also tie ribbons to branches. Make sure the markers are easy to see and follow. Once you've set up the trail, have a friend or family member follow it. See if they can find their way using your markers. This exercise helps you practice creating clear and effective trail markers. It also shows you how useful they can be in guiding others.

Trail markers are a simple yet powerful tool for navigation. They help you find your way and stay safe while exploring. By learning how to create and use them, you gain confidence in your ability to navigate the wilderness. These skills are valuable for any adventurer.

CHAPTER EIGHT

READING THE WEATHER

P icture this: you're at a park, enjoying a sunny day with your family. Suddenly, the sky changes, and you see different shapes and colors in the clouds above. These changes can tell you a lot about the weather. Knowing how to read the sky can help you prepare for what's coming. It's like having your own weather forecast right above you. This chapter will teach you how to understand clouds and weather patterns. These skills can help you stay safe and enjoy your time outdoors even more.

UNDERSTANDING CLOUDS AND WEATHER PATTERNS

Clouds are not just fluffy shapes in the sky. They tell you a lot about the weather. For example, cumulus clouds are fluffy and white. These clouds often mean nice weather. You see them on sunny days, and they look like cotton balls floating in the sky. They are not very tall, which usually means you can expect good weather for the day. When you see these clouds, you can relax and enjoy outdoor activities without worrying about rain.

Not all clouds bring good news. Stratus clouds are gray and spread out like a blanket across the sky. They can bring light rain or drizzle. These clouds cover the sky in a gray layer, often making the day gloomy. Having a raincoat or umbrella handy is a good idea when you see stratus clouds. These clouds don't usually bring heavy storms but can make everything damp and cool.

Cirrus clouds are high, wispy clouds that look like feathers. Cirrus clouds look like cotton balls that have been pulled apart. They are very high up in the sky, often meaning the weather might change soon. These clouds are made of ice crystals, not water droplets. When you see cirrus clouds, it's a sign that the weather could change in the next day or so. Maybe a storm is coming, or maybe it will just get cooler. Either way, it's good to pay attention to these clouds.

Cumulonimbus clouds are imposing giants in the cloud family, known for their towering presence that can signal the onset of thunderstorms. These large clouds extend high into the atmosphere, often appearing to have a flat base and sometimes also a flat top. When cumulonimbus clouds are coming your way in the sky, it clearly indicates that a storm, complete with heavy rainfall, thunder, lightning, and possibly even hail, is imminent. Spotting these clouds means it's time to seek shelter and prepare for inclement weather.

Observing cloud formations can be fun and educational. Start by noting the height and shape of the clouds. Are they low and spread out, or high and wispy? Look at how the clouds change throughout the day. Do they get darker or thicker? Do new types of clouds appear? By paying attention to these details, you can learn to predict the weather just by looking at the sky.

Weather patterns and systems also play a big role in the weather you experience. High-pressure systems usually bring clear skies and stable weather. These systems push clouds away, making the sky clear and blue. When you see clear skies, it's often because of a high-pressure system. These systems are great for outdoor activities because they usually mean good weather.

Low-pressure systems are different. They often lead to clouds, rain, and storms. These systems pull in air and moisture, forming clouds and rain. When you see a lot of clouds and feel the air getting cooler, it's probably because of a low-pressure system. These systems can bring rain, snow, or even thunderstorms. Knowing the difference between high and low-pressure systems can help you understand why the weather changes.

Try keeping a weather journal to help you get better at reading the sky. Each day, write down what the clouds look like and what the weather is like. Note the types of clouds you see and any changes you notice. Draw pictures of the different cloud types and write a few words about what they might mean. Over time, you'll start to see patterns and get better at predicting the weather.

Understanding clouds and weather patterns is like having a secret weather prediction tool. By learning to read the sky, you can prepare for what's coming and stay safe. Plus, it's a fun way to connect with nature and understand the world around you. So next time you're outside, take a moment to look up at the sky and see what the clouds are telling you.

PREDICTING WEATHER USING NATURAL SIGNS

Imagine you're out on a hike, and you notice birds flying low to the ground. This might mean a storm is coming. Birds often fly lower when the air pressure drops before a storm. They do this to stay safe and avoid turbulence in the higher air. Watching bird behavior can give you clues about the weather. If you see birds flying close to the ground, finding shelter or heading back to a safer location is a good idea.

Have you ever heard frogs croaking loudly at night? Frogs often make more noise before it rains. They do this because they use the rain to mate and lay eggs in water. When you hear frogs being extra loud, it could mean that rain is on the way. This is a useful tip, especially if you're camping. It helps you prepare for wet weather by setting up your tent or finding a dry spot to wait out the rain.

Ants can also give you hints about the weather. When you see ants building their mounds higher, it usually means heavy rain is coming. Ants do this to protect their homes from getting flooded. They work hard to make sure their tunnels stay dry. You can get a heads-up on heavy rain by watching ants and noticing when they build higher mounds. This gives you time to prepare, like putting on rain gear or finding a waterproof cover for your backpack.

Plants are another natural indicator of weather changes. Pinecones, for instance, are great at predicting rain. Pinecones close up when the air becomes humid, or rain is coming. They do this to protect their seeds from getting wet. Next time you see pinecones, take a look at whether they are open or closed. If they are closed, it's a sign that the weather might get wet soon. This can help you decide if you need to cut your outdoor activities short or find shelter.

Flowers can also tell you about the weather. Many flowers close or droop when rain is approaching. They do this to protect their pollen from getting washed away. If you see flowers closing up or looking droopy, it's a good idea to prepare for rain. This might mean packing up your picnic or putting on a rain jacket. Observing plants and their reactions to the weather can help you stay dry and comfortable.

Wind direction and speed are important weather clues. When the wind shifts direction, it can mean a change in weather patterns. For example, if the wind suddenly starts blowing from a different direction, it might mean a storm is coming. Pay attention to which way the wind is blowing and notice if it changes. A sudden increase in wind speed often happens before storms. If you feel the wind picking up, it's a sign that you should find shelter soon. Wind can be a powerful indicator of changing weather, so paying attention to it is important.

To practice using natural signs for weather prediction, observe and record animal behavior before and after weather changes. Keep a small notebook and write down what you see. Note the behavior of birds, frogs, and ants. Write about how they act before rain and compare it to how they act on sunny days. This will help you see patterns and understand how animals react to weather changes.

You can also observe changes in plant behavior in different weather conditions. Take notes on how pine cones and flowers look on sunny days versus rainy days. Draw pictures of the plants and write a few words about their appearance. This helps you remember what to look for and makes it easier to predict the weather based on plant behavior.

Learning to read natural signs can be a fun and useful skill. It helps you understand the world around you and stay prepared for different weather conditions. By paying attention to animals, plants, and the wind, you can become a weather expert in your own right. This makes your outdoor adventures safer and more enjoyable. So, next time you're outside, take a moment to observe the natural signs around you and see what they tell you about the weather.

PREPARING FOR RAIN AND STORMS

Imagine you're camping with your family, and you notice the sky getting darker. The wind picks up, and you feel a sudden drop in temperature. These are signs that a storm is coming. Darkening skies and increasing cloud cover often mean rain or a storm is coming. If you see the sky turning a deep gray or black, it's time to prepare. Thunder and lightning in the distance are also clear signs. If you hear thunder, it means lightning is nearby, even if you can't see it yet. When you feel a sudden drop in temperature, it usually means that cold air from the storm is moving in. These cues can help you get ready before the storm hits.

Setting up a campsite for rain involves some thoughtful planning. First, make sure your tent is on high ground. This helps avoid flooding. Next, set up a tarp shelter to stay dry. Stretch a tarp above your tent or sleeping area to create a waterproof roof. Secure the corners tightly with ropes and stakes. This keeps the tarp from blowing away in the wind. Dig small trenches around your tent to divert water. These trenches guide rainwater away from your sleeping area, keeping it dry. Make sure to secure loose items around the campsite. Strong winds can blow away gear like chairs, cooking utensils, and even backpacks. Tie down or store these items inside your tent or under the tarp.

Personal preparation for rain is just as important. To ensure you remain dry and comfortable, it's essential to wear waterproof clothing and sturdy, waterproof footwear. Opt for a breathable, waterproof jacket and pants. These garments are specifically designed to prevent water from penetrating while allowing moisture from your body to escape, keeping you dry from both external and internal sources of moisture. Waterproof boots or shoes are also crucial; they protect your feet from getting wet, which is vital for maintaining warmth and comfort.

Additionally, it is wise to carry a rain poncho or an extra water-proof jacket in your backpack as a backup. These lightweight and compact items provide a quick, effective layer of protection against unforeseen downpours. Equipping yourself with the appropriate waterproof gear is a straightforward yet critical step in enjoying your outdoor adventures, even when the weather turns wet.

During outdoor adventures, you also need to be prepared for lightning. Here's how you can protect yourself if you're caught in a sudden lightning storm. The moment you sense a storm approaching, prioritize finding shelter. Sturdy buildings or vehicles offer the best protection against the elements. Avoid open fields or high ground, as these areas increase your risk during lightning strikes. Lightning seeks the path of least resistance to the ground, often striking tall objects. Stay clear of isolated tall trees, poles, or metal structures. If you find yourself in an open area with no possibility of reaching shelter, minimize your contact with the ground to reduce the likelihood of being struck by ground current from a lightning strike. Crouch down on the balls of your feet, keeping your feet together and your head tucked down. Never lie flat on the ground. Water conducts electricity, so avoid lakes, rivers, and wet areas. If you're swimming or boating, get to land and find shelter immediately. Preparation, awareness, and quick action are your best defenses against the unpredictable nature of storms. Remember, your safety is the most important part of any adventure. Always err on the side of caution when storms threaten.

Knowing how to recognize the signs of an approaching storm and how to prepare can keep you safe and dry. Watching the sky, feeling the temperature, and listening for thunder are all valuable skills. Setting up your campsite to handle rain and using the right clothing and gear make a big difference. And most importantly, knowing where to find shelter during a storm can protect you from harm.

STAYING SAFE IN EXTREME WEATHER CONDITIONS

Extreme weather can be dangerous. It's important to know how to stay safe. Let's talk about different types of extreme weather and what risks they bring. Heatwaves are periods of very hot weather that can make you feel tired and weak. The biggest risks during a heatwave are dehydration and heatstroke. Dehydration happens when you lose more water than you take in. This can make you feel dizzy and thirsty. If it gets worse, it can cause serious health problems. Heatstroke is even more dangerous. It happens when your body gets too hot and can't cool down. This can cause confusion, headaches, and even fainting.

Another type of extreme weather is cold snaps. These are periods of freezing weather. The main risks during a cold snap are frostbite and hypothermia. Frostbite happens when your skin and the tissue underneath freeze. This usually affects fingers, toes, and the nose. It can cause numbness and change the color of your skin. Hypothermia is when your body temperature drops too low. This can make you shiver and feel very tired. If it gets worse, it can make you confused and even unconscious. Both frostbite and hypothermia are serious and need quick treatment.

Thunderstorms are also dangerous. They bring heavy rain, strong winds, and lightning. Lightning strikes can cause burns and even be deadly. The strong winds can knock down trees and power lines. It's important to seek shelter during a thunderstorm to avoid these dangers. Flash floods are sudden floods that happen when there is a lot of rain in a short time. The fast-moving water can be very powerful. It can sweep away cars, trees, and even people.

Flash floods can happen with little warning, so knowing how to stay safe is important.

There are ways to stay cool and hydrated when the weather is extremely hot. Drink plenty of water. Avoid sugary drinks like soda, as they can make you more thirsty. Water is the best choice. Seek shade whenever you can. Look for natural shade under trees or construct a temporary shade using a tarp or any available materials. Staying out of the sun helps keep your body cool. Wear light, breathable clothing. This type of clothing helps your body stay cool. Take breaks often. Avoid doing too much activity during the hottest parts of the day, usually between 10 a.m. and 4 p.m. If you have to be outside, try to rest in the shade as much as possible.

Cold weather requires different preparations. Dressing in layers is the best way to stay warm. Start with a base layer, like thermal underwear. Add a middle layer, like a fleece jacket. Finish with an outer layer, like a waterproof coat. This helps trap heat and keeps you warm. Wear a hat, gloves, and insulated footwear. A lot of body heat is lost through the head and hands, so keeping these areas covered is important. Moving around helps maintain circulation and warmth. If you start to feel cold, try walking around or doing some exercises to warm up. Find or build a shelter to shield yourself from the wind and retain warmth. You can use branches, leaves, or snow to construct a barrier against the cold. Wrap yourself in a sleeping bag or blanket if available, focusing on insulating your body's core to preserve vital heat. Eating high-energy foods can also help your body generate additional heat.

In all extreme weather scenarios, it's critical to signal for help. Use a whistle, a mirror, or any item that can make you more visible or audible to rescuers. Stay in one place to conserve energy and make it easier for help to find you. If you're with others, stay together to share warmth and resources. Use materials from your surroundings for additional insulation, such as stuffing leaves, pine needles, or even paper between layers of clothing. Remember, in extreme weather conditions, staying calm, thinking clearly, and taking proactive steps to protect yourself can significantly increase your chances of survival. Preparation and knowledge are your best defenses when facing the scorching heat, the biting cold, or any other severe weather.

Staying safe in extreme weather means being prepared and knowing what to do. Whether it's a heatwave, cold snap, thunderstorm, or flash flood, having the right knowledge and tools can keep you safe. Now that you know how to handle extreme weather, you're ready for anything nature throws at you. Next, we will talk about something just as important—how to stay calm and think clearly when facing a challenging situation in the wild.

CHAPTER NINE

SURVIVAL MINDSET AND RESILIENCE

I magine you're hiking through a dense forest. You've been walking for hours, and suddenly, you realize you're not sure which direction to go. Your heart starts to race, and you feel a wave of panic. Staying calm in the moment is crucial. It helps you think clearly and make smart decisions. When you panic, your mind gets cloudy, and you might make mistakes that put you in more danger. Calmness allows you to assess the situation, figure out the best plan, and take action. Panic wastes your energy, and you need every bit of strength to handle the challenges ahead.

STAYING CALM UNDER PRESSURE

Staying calm is one of the most important skills in survival situations. When you're calm, you can think clearly and make better decisions. Clear thinking helps you find solutions to problems and avoid making mistakes. For example, if you're lost, staying calm allows you to remember the steps to find your way back. It helps you use the skills you've learned, like reading a map or using a compass. Panic, on the other hand, can make you forget these important skills. Energy conservation is another reason to stay calm. Panic can waste the energy that you need to survive. When you panic, your heart rate increases, and you breathe faster. This uses up more energy and can make you tired quickly. By staying calm, you can conserve your energy and use it when you really need it.

There are simple techniques that you can use to help you stay calm. First, practice deep, slow breathing: it's a straightforward yet powerful method. When you feel panic starting, stop and take a deep breath in through your nose. Gently inhale through your nose, allowing your chest and belly to rise as you fill your lungs with air. Hold this breath momentarily, then slowly release it through your mouth. Repeat the slow inhale and exhale process five times. This cycle of deep, purposeful breaths slows your heart rate, allowing your body and mind to relax. The second method is visualization. This involves finding a quiet moment to close your eyes and imagine a calm, happy place. Visualize yourself in this peaceful setting, feeling safe and grounded. This practice can significantly diminish stress levels, helping you reclaim your sense of control. The last method we'll discuss is practicing positive self-talk. In moments of uncertainty, be your own cheerleader. Use confident, uplifting phrases like, "I've got this" or "I'm equipped to handle this situation." This boosts your confidence and keeps your focus laser-sharp on the solutions rather than the problems.

Recognizing signs of panic early can help you address them before they get worse. Pay attention to your body. An increased heart rate is one of the first signs of panic. If you notice your heart beating faster, it's a signal to start calming techniques. Racing thoughts are another sign. When your mind jumps from one worry to another, it's harder to focus. Recognizing these signs helps you take action to calm down before panic takes over.

Practical Exercise: Calming Techniques

Practice calming techniques regularly to make them more effective. Start with daily deep breathing sessions. Spend a few minutes each day practicing deep breaths. This helps you get used to the technique so you can use it easily when needed. Try mindfulness exercises. Spend a few moments focusing on your senses. What can you see, hear, smell, taste, and touch? This helps ground you in the present moment and reduces anxiety.

BUILDING CONFIDENCE AND SELF-RELIANCE

Picture yourself in the woods, faced with the task of setting up a shelter before nightfall. Confidence in your skills can make all the difference. When you feel confident, you make decisions more easily. Confidence helps you choose the best spot for your shelter and figure out which materials to use. It also encourages you to take action without second-guessing yourself. This is important because, in survival situations, quick and accurate decisions can keep you safe.

Confidence also encourages you to take the initiative. Instead of waiting for someone else to tell you what to do, you jump right in. You gather sticks and leaves for your shelter. You clear the area of any sharp rocks or branches. This proactive behavior helps you stay ahead of challenges. It also makes you feel more in control of the situation. Taking charge makes you feel more capable and ready to tackle whatever comes next.

Building confidence is a journey that requires consistent practice and dedication. It doesn't happen overnight but grows with each new challenge you overcome. Start this journey by focusing on mastering a single skill, no matter how basic it may seem. Begin with something accessible, like learning to tie various types of knots. Dedicate time to practice these knots repeatedly until you can easily tie them without looking. Mastering a fundamental skill will be a stepping stone, boosting your confidence and preparing you for more complex tasks.

Once you have mastered one survival skill, gradually expand your skill set to include other survival techniques, such as fire-starting. Experiment with different methods, like using a magnifying glass on sunny days or striking flint and steel when it's overcast. Each new skill you master adds to your survival toolkit and significantly enhances your confidence in your abilities. To further build your confidence, role-play scenarios with friends or family members. These simulated exercises can range from navigating back to camp using only a compass and map to collaboratively constructing a shelter from natural materials. Such activities solidify your skills through practical application and improve your problem-solving abilities and teamwork skills. The positive feedback and encouragement from participating in these group challenges will further bolster your self-esteem. Another effective strategy for developing self-reliance and confidence is to undertake solo challenges. Under supervision and in safe conditions, attempt tasks such as setting up a tent by yourself or preparing a meal outdoors. These activities encourage independence and teach you to trust in your capabilities.

Additionally, incorporate daily self-sufficiency tasks into your routine, like organizing your gear or planning a hiking route. These tasks, though small, are significant steps toward building a resilient and self-reliant mindset. It's also crucial to acknowledge and celebrate your progress. Maintain a journal to record your achievements, no matter how minor they may seem. This could include successfully starting a fire with a new method or building a shelter that withstands the elements. Reflecting on these accomplishments will remind you of how far you've come and motivate you to continue learning and growing. Lastly, consider setting up a personal reward system to help you achieve your goals. Rewards could be as simple as a favorite snack after completing a challenging hike or extra leisure time following a successful skill demonstration. This system makes the learning process more enjoyable. It serves as an incentive to push your limits and achieve new milestones. By systematically mastering skills, engaging in practical exercises, undertaking challenges, and recognizing your achievements, your confidence and self-reliance in survival situations steadily increase. This foundation of confidence empowers you to face the wilderness with determination and the knowledge that you are equipped to overcome whatever challenges you may encounter.

PROBLEM-SOLVING IN TOUGH SITUATIONS

Imagine you're out in the woods and suddenly realize you've lost your way. You don't panic because you know how to solve problems. Problem-solving skills are crucial in survival. They help you adapt to changing situations. This means you can handle whatever comes your way. When you face a challenge, you need to think quickly and creatively. Problem-solving helps you do that. It encourages you to use the resources you have in smart ways. You might find new uses for everyday items. This creativity can make a big difference in tough situations.

Let's break down the steps for effective problem-solving. First, define the problem. Clearly identify what's wrong. For example, if you're lost, the problem is finding your way back. Next, brainstorm solutions. Think of as many ideas as you can. Don't worry if some seem silly. The goal is to come up with options. Once you have your list, evaluate your options. Weigh the pros and cons of each solution. Ask yourself questions like, "Which path seems safer?" or "Do I have enough supplies for this route?" Finally, choose the best solution and take action. Pick the option that seems most likely to work and go for it. Being decisive helps you move forward.

Creative thinking is a big part of solving problems. Sometimes, the obvious solution isn't the best one. You should think outside the box. For example, you could use a magnifying glass to start a fire if you're out of matches. Or, if you need shelter but don't have a tent, you could build one from leaves and branches. Finding multiple uses for common items is also helpful. A bandana can be a head cover, a water filter, or even a sling for an injured arm. This kind of thinking helps you make the most of what you have.

Problem-Solving Activities

Practicing problem-solving can make you better at it. Let's try some puzzle-solving scenarios. Imagine you're stranded on an island. You need to find fresh water. Think of different ways to get it. You could collect rainwater, dig a hole to find groundwater or build a solar still. Write down your ideas and evaluate them. Which one seems easiest? Which one would take the least time? Choose the best option and explain why it's the best. This exercise helps you practice thinking through problems and finding solutions.

Group activities are another great way to practice problem-solving. Gather some friends and try a collaborative challenge. For example, pretend you're all shipwrecked and need to build a raft. Work together to find materials and figure out how to put them together. Each person can contribute ideas. This helps you learn to work as a team and solve problems together. It also shows you that different perspectives can lead to better solutions.

Problem-solving in tough situations is about staying flexible and creative. It helps you adapt to changes and use your resources wisely. By practicing these skills, you become more prepared for any challenges you face. Defining the problem, brainstorming solutions, evaluating options, and taking action are all steps that guide you through the process. Creative thinking and using available materials in new ways make you resourceful. Practicing with puzzles and group activities helps you get better at solving problems. This makes you ready for whatever comes your way in the wilderness.

STAYING MOTIVATED IN THE WILD

Imagine you're out in the wilderness, and you've been hiking all day. Your legs are tired, and you feel like you can't take another step. This is when motivation becomes your best friend. Staying motivated is crucial in survival situations. It helps you keep your energy up and stay focused. When you're motivated, you can push through tough times. It gives you the strength to keep going, even when things get hard. Motivation encourages you to persist, no matter what challenges you face.

One way to stay motivated is to set small goals. Break down big tasks into smaller, manageable steps. For example, if you need to build a shelter, focus on gathering materials first. Then, work on setting up the frame. Finally, add the covering. Completing each small step gives you a sense of accomplishment, which keeps you motivated to move on to the next step. It's like climbing a ladder one rung at a time. Each small goal brings you closer to the bigger goal.

Finding inspiration can also boost your motivation. Think about stories of other people who have faced similar challenges and succeeded. Remember quotes that uplift you. For example, "Stay strong, even when it's tough." Use positive affirmations to remind yourself that you can do it. Tell yourself, "I am capable," and "I can handle this." These positive thoughts can lift your spirits and keep you going.

Maintaining a routine helps provide structure in your day. When you have a routine, you know what to expect. This makes it easier to stay focused and motivated. Create a daily routine that includes time for rest, work, and fun. For example, start your day with a small task, like gathering firewood. Take breaks to rest and eat. Spend some time on a fun activity, like exploring your surroundings. Having a routine helps you stay organized and makes the day feel more manageable.

Sometimes, despite your best efforts, you might feel discouraged. It's important to recognize and manage these feelings. It's okay to feel down sometimes. Acknowledge your feelings and remind yourself that it's normal. The key is to keep going. Take a moment to rest and recharge. Talk to a friend or an adult if you're feeling low. Sharing your feelings can help lighten the load. They can offer support and encouragement, which can boost your motivation.

Motivation helps you stay energized and focused and encourages you to keep going, even when things get tough. You can boost your motivation by setting small goals, finding inspiration, and maintaining a routine. Recognizing and managing discouragement helps you stay on track. With these strategies, you'll be ready to face any challenges and keep moving forward.

CHAPTER TEN
REAL-LIFE SURVIVAL STORIES AND CHALLENGES

THE BOY WHO SURVIVED THE DESERT

I magine being alone in the vast desert, with the scorching sun beating down on you. You have no shade, and your water bottle is empty. This might sound like a scary movie, but for one young boy, it was real life. In this chapter, we'll dive into his incredible story and learn the survival skills that helped him make it through.

One day, a boy named Jake found himself in a tough spot. While exploring near his home in Arizona, he wandered too far into the desert. Suddenly, he realized he was lost. The desert is a harsh place. The heat is intense, and water is hard to find. Jake knew he had to stay calm and use his survival skills to stay alive.

The first challenge Jake faced was the extreme heat. The desert sun can be brutal, making it hard to think and move. Jake knew he needed to find shade quickly to avoid overheating. He spotted a large rock formation and headed towards it. The rock provided some relief from the sun's rays. Jake stayed close to the rock, using its shadow to keep cool as much as possible. He also remembered to conserve his energy. Instead of walking around aimlessly, he sat still during the hottest part of the day. This helped him stay cool and saved his strength.

Finding water in the desert is a huge challenge. Jake knew that wandering around without a plan could make things worse. He looked around for any signs of water. He noticed some animal tracks in the sand. Animals often know where to find water. Jake followed the tracks, hoping they would lead him to a water source. After a while, he saw some birds circling in the sky. Birds often hang around water sources, too. Jake kept moving in that direction, staying alert for any signs of water.

Jake's efforts paid off. He found a small, muddy puddle. It wasn't much, but it was better than nothing. He used his shirt to filter the water, making it safer to drink. This simple trick helped him stay hydrated and gave him the strength to keep going.

Jake returned to the rock formation he found earlier, choosing the rocks as a good place to stay put while waiting for help. There weren't enough natural materials around to use for a signal fire, and Jake didn't have a whistle to signal for help. Jake got creative and tested banging things against the rocks to make loud noises. He discovered that his belt buckle made the loudest noise when he banged it against one of the rocks. Jake struck his belt buckle against the rock three times, waited a few seconds, and repeated three more times. Rescuers were able to follow the noise and saved Jake.

Throughout his ordeal, Jake stayed calm and remained focused. He knew that panicking would only make things worse. Jake used mental strategies to stay positive. He thought about his family and how happy they would be when he made it back home. He also reminded himself of the survival skills he had learned. This positive mindset helped him stay motivated and hopeful.

Jake's story teaches us some valuable lessons. First, finding shade and conserving energy is crucial in hot environments. Look for natural shelters like rocks or trees. Stay still during the hottest part of the day to avoid overheating. Second, following animal tracks can lead you to water. Animals know where to find water sources, so pay attention to their movements. Filtering water with a piece of cloth can make it safer to drink. Third, staying in one location and creating signals for rescuers to lead them to your location will allow help to reach you the fastest.

Here are some practical tips inspired by Jake's story:

Practical Tips for Desert Survival

Finding Water in Arid Environments:

- Follow animal tracks. Animals often lead to water sources.
- Look for birds circling in the sky. They usually stay near water.
- Use a piece of cloth to filter muddy water.

Staying Cool and Conserving Energy:

- Find shade under rocks, trees, or bushes.
- Rest during the hottest part of the day.
- Move slowly and avoid overexertion.

Signaling for Help:

- Find a safe location.
- Create signals that rescuers can see or hear.
- Stay in that safe location while continuing to signal for help.

Jake's story shows us that staying calm and using your survival skills can make all the difference. Whether you're in the desert, the woods, or any other wild place, these skills can help you stay safe and find your way back home.

THE GIRL WHO FOUND HER WAY HOME

Imagine you're hiking with your class, exploring a beautiful forest. You're having a great time, but then you realize you've wandered off the path while looking at some cool plants. You look around, and your group is nowhere to be seen. This is exactly what happened to a girl named Emma. She got separated from her group during a hike. The forest was dense, and every direction looked the same. Emma knew she had to stay calm and use her navigation skills to find her way back home.

Emma had learned about using landmarks to stay oriented. She remembered that there was a big, unique tree near the trail. The tree had an odd shape, almost like it was twisted. She decided to look for that tree. As she walked, she noticed other natural features like a small stream and a large rock. These landmarks helped her keep track of where she was. Emma knew that if she kept these landmarks in mind, she could avoid walking in circles and getting even more lost.

Navigating through the dense forest was tough. The trees were close together, and it was hard to see very far ahead. Emma remembered that streams often lead to larger bodies of water or even to places where people live. She decided to follow the small stream. The stream was narrow, and the water was clear. She walked along the edge, making sure not to slip on the wet rocks. Following the stream gave her a sense of direction and a bit of hope.

Emma also knew the importance of staying safe while navigating. She found safe places to rest along the way. Whenever Emma felt tired, she looked for a spot under a large tree or near a rock that provided some protection. She made sure to stay hydrated by drinking water from the stream. To keep it safe to drink, Emma used a piece of cloth she had in her backpack to filter out any dirt or small particles. Staying hydrated kept her energy up and helped her think clearly.

As night approached, Emma knew she needed to keep warm. The temperature in the forest could drop quickly after the sun went down. She gathered dry leaves and grass to create some insulation. She stuffed the leaves inside her jacket and pants to help keep her body heat close. Emma also found a small hollow under a tree where she could curl up and be protected from the wind. These steps helped her stay warm and get some rest, even though she was still worried about finding her way back. Emma also knew that staying in one place would make it easier for help to find her. A search party found Emma overnight while she was sheltered in the hollow of the tree.

Inspired by Emma's story, here are some practical exercises you can try to practice your own navigation skills. One fun activity is setting up a mini orienteering course in a local park. Use a map of the park and mark out a few key landmarks like a big tree, a bench, or a playground. Then, create a route that connects these landmarks. Try to follow the route using the map, paying attention to how the landmarks look in real life. This exercise helps you get better at reading maps and using natural features to stay on track.

Another great practice is following natural landmarks on a hike. Next time you go on a hike with your family or friends, pick out a few landmarks along the way. These could be a large rock, a stream, or a unique tree. As you hike, remember these landmarks and try to remember their order. On the way back, see if you can recognize the landmarks and use them to guide your way. This practice helps you get used to noticing and remembering important features in your surroundings.

Practical Tips for Forest Survival

Look for Landmarks

- Landmarks that you see on your way into the forest can help guide you out.
- If you become lost, memorizing landmarks can tell you if you're walking in circles.

Sources of Water can Lead to People

- A stream or river will likely lead to buildings or towns.
- Flowing water is likely safer to drink than stagnant water from a lake or pond.
- Be careful when walking along a stream to avoid slipping on wet rocks and injuring yourself.

Finding Shelter and Staying Warm

- Look for natural enclosures that will block the wind and rain.
- Leaves and grass stuffed into your clothes will act as insulation against the cold.
- Staying in one location will make it easier for rescuers to find you.

Emma's story shows us that staying calm and using your navigation skills can help you find your way home, even in a dense forest.

By paying attention to landmarks, following natural features like streams, and staying safe, you can navigate through tough situations. Practicing these skills in a fun and safe way helps you get ready for any adventure.

THE FAMILY RESCUED BY THEIR SIGNAL FIRE

Imagine you're on a family camping trip in the mountains. The scenery is beautiful, but there's no cell service, and you're far from any town. Suddenly, your car breaks down on a remote road. You realize you're stranded. This is exactly what happened to the Brown family. Without any way to call for help, they had to rely on their survival skills to get rescued.

The Browns knew they had to attract attention. They decided to build a signal fire. A signal fire is a fire that produces a lot of smoke, which can be seen from far away. The family chose a spot on a hill where the fire would be visible to anyone passing by, even from a distance. They collected dry wood to start the fire and green branches to create thick smoke. The green branches are critical because they produce a lot of smoke when they burn. This smoke can be seen from miles away, making it an effective signal for help.

Building the fire required teamwork. Dad gathered the dry wood, Mom collected the green branches, and the kids helped arrange the materials. They built a small teepee structure with dry wood and placed the green branches on top. Using a fire starter, they ignited the dry wood. As the fire grew, they added more green branches. Soon, thick, white smoke rose into the sky. They kept the fire going, making sure the smoke remained steady.

Teamwork played a huge role in their survival. Dividing tasks made the job easier and quicker. Each family member had a role, which kept everyone involved and focused. They also supported each other emotionally. When someone felt scared or worried, the others offered encouragement. This emotional support was just as important as the physical work. It kept their spirits up and helped them stay hopeful.

Inspired by the Browns' story, here are some practical tips and activities for you to practice your signaling skills. One activity is building a small, safe signal fire under adult supervision. Choose a clear, open area for the fire. Gather dry wood and green branches. Build a small teepee structure with dry wood and place the green branches on top. Light the fire and watch how the smoke rises. Practice adding green branches to keep the smoke thick. This hands-on experience helps you understand how to build an effective signal fire.

Another fun activity is creating different types of signals. You can use a mirror or a whistle to signal for help. Practice using a mirror to reflect sunlight. Hold the mirror in one hand and aim the reflected light at a distant point. This creates a bright flash that can be seen from far away. Use a whistle to make loud, distinct sounds. Three short blasts are the international signal of distress. Practicing these signals helps you get comfortable using them in real situations.

In case you are ever stranded, here are some tips to keep in mind:

Choosing a Visible Location:

- Find an open area, such as a hill or a clearing.
- Make sure the location is visible from the air and from a distance.

Using Green Branches for Smoke:

- Collect green branches from trees or bushes.
- Place them on top of the fire to create thick, white smoke.

Teamwork and Emotional Support:

- Divide tasks among family members.
- Offer encouragement and support to keep everyone motivated.

Building a Signal Fire:

- Gather dry wood for the base.
- Arrange the wood in a teepee structure.
- Add green branches to create smoke.
- Light the fire and keep adding green branches to maintain the smoke.

Creating Different Types of Signals:

- Use a mirror to reflect sunlight and create a bright flash.
- Blow a whistle in three short blasts to signal for help.

Practicing these skills can prepare you for any situation. Whether building a signal fire or using a mirror and whistle, these techniques can help you attract attention and get rescued. So the next time you're out exploring, remember the Brown family's story and the importance of teamwork and signaling for help.

CHAPTER ELEVEN

FUN AND INTERACTIVE SURVIVAL ACTIVITIES

I magine you're out in the backyard with your friends. The sun is shining, and the air is full of excitement. You're about to start a scavenger hunt, a fun game where you search for items hidden around you. But this isn't just any scavenger hunt. It's a survival skills scavenger hunt! You'll look for items that can help you survive in the wild. This game is not only fun but also helps you practice important skills. Let's get started!

SURVIVAL SKILLS SCAVENGER HUNT

A scavenger hunt is a game where you search for specific items. In a survival skills scavenger hunt, you look for things that you can use in the wild. It's a great way to practice your survival skills while having fun. You can do this hunt in your backyard, at a park, or even on a camping trip. The goal is to find items that can help you survive, like tinder for starting a fire, materials for building a shelter, or edible plants.

First, you need to create a list of survival-related items to find. Different types of tinder are a good start. Look for dry leaves, pine needles, and birch bark. These materials catch fire easily and are great for starting a fire. Next, search for natural materials for shelter building. Sticks, rocks, and leaves are perfect items. Sticks can be used to make the frame of a shelter. Rocks can help hold things in place. Leaves can provide insulation. Finally, look for edible plants or berries. Dandelions, clover, and blackberries are common and easy to identify. They can provide food if you're out in the wild.

Setting up the scavenger hunt is easy. First, mark safe and accessible areas for the hunt. Make sure everyone knows where they can go and where they should avoid. This keeps everyone safe and ensures a fun experience. Next, divide the kids into teams. Working in teams makes the hunt more fun and encourages collaboration. Each team gets a list of items to find. Set a time limit for the hunt. When time's up, see which team found the most items.

This scavenger hunt has many educational benefits. It encourages observation and identification skills. You'll learn to spot useful items in your environment. This is an important part of survival. The hunt also promotes teamwork and problem-solving. You'll work with your team to find items and figure out how to use them. This helps you think creatively and work well with others.

Organizing and conducting the scavenger hunt is simple. Start by choosing a safe location. Parks and backyards are great options. Create a list of items for the kids to find. Make sure the items are common in the area. Divide the kids into teams and explain the rules. Set a time limit and let the hunt begin. Monitor the kids to ensure they stay within the boundaries and stay safe.

Scavenger Hunt Checklist

- Different types of tinder: dry leaves, pine needles, birch bark
- Natural materials for shelter building: sticks, rocks, leaves
- Edible plants or berries: dandelions, clover, blackberries

Scavenger hunts are a fun way to practice survival skills. They help you learn to identify useful items in your environment and work as a team. Plus, they're a great way to enjoy the outdoors. So grab your friends, make a list, and start your own survival skills scavenger hunt. You'll have fun and learn important skills at the same time.

BUILDING A MINIATURE SURVIVAL SHELTER MODEL

Imagine you are deep in the woods, and the sun is setting. You need to build a shelter quickly to stay safe and warm. But how do you start? Building a miniature shelter model can help you understand the steps. It's like building a small version of what you'll make in the wild. By using natural materials, you learn how to gather and put together the right stuff. This skill is useful when you need to build a natural shelter. It's like practicing with a toy before using the real thing.

To build your miniature shelters, you'll need some simple materials. Gather twigs, leaves, and small rocks from your backyard or a park. These will act as the main structure and covering for your shelter. You'll also need string or twine to secure the materials together. These items are easy to find and perfect for making small models. You can also use small pieces of bark or pine needles for extra detail. These materials help make the models more realistic and sturdy.

Let's start with a mini lean-to shelter. Take a long twig and place it horizontally between two small rocks. This will act as the main support. Lean smaller twigs against the main twig to form a frame. Make sure the twigs are close together to provide good coverage. Next, cover the frame with leaves. This will act as insulation and protection from the wind. Use string or twine to secure the twigs and leaves in place. Your mini lean-to shelter is now complete!

Creating a small debris hut is also fun and useful. Start by finding a sturdy, short twig to act as the central ridge pole. Place it between two small rocks or prop it up with other twigs. Lean smaller twigs against the ridge pole to form a frame. Pile leaves and other debris over the frame to create insulation. The more leaves you add, the warmer the shelter will be. Secure everything with string or twine. Your debris hut is now ready to provide warmth and protection.

A tiny tarp shelter is another great model to build. Find a small piece of cloth or plastic to act as your tarp. Stretch the tarp between two small rocks or twigs to create a roof. Use string or twine to secure the tarp in place. Make sure the tarp is tight and doesn't sag. This will help keep rain and wind out. You can add small rocks to the tarp's corners for extra stability. Your mini tarp shelter is now set up and ready to use.

Add some extra touches to make your models more realistic and sturdy. Layer leaves on top of your shelters for better insulation. This will make them warmer and more effective. Use small pebbles to stabilize the structures. Place the pebbles around the base of the shelters to hold everything in place. This helps prevent the shelters from collapsing. You can add small details like tiny bark or pine needles for a more realistic look. These touches make your models look and work like real shelters.

Building miniature shelter models is a great way to practice and learn. You get to see how different materials work together. You also learn the basic steps of shelter building. This practice helps you feel more confident when you need to build a real shelter. Plus, it's a fun and creative activity you can do with friends or family. So grab your materials and start building. You'll have a great time and learn important skills along the way.

FIRST AID ROLE-PLAYING SCENARIOS

Imagine you and your friends are out on a hike. Suddenly, one of your friends trips and falls. They scrape their knee and start to cry. You know you need to help, but how? Role-playing can help you practice first-aid skills. It's like acting out different scenarios, so you know what to do in real life. You can simulate common outdoor injuries and learn how to treat them. By assigning roles, one person can be the injured friend, and another can be the first responder. This makes the practice realistic and fun.

Let's start with some example scenarios. One common situation is treating a cut or scrape on the leg. You can draw a pretend cut on your friend's leg using a red marker. The first responder can then clean the wound with a wet wipe, apply an antiseptic, and put on a bandage. Another scenario could be handling an insect bite or sting. Your friend can pretend to be stung by a bee. The first responder can use tweezers to remove the stinger, clean the area, and apply an anti-itch cream. Making and using a sling for a sprained arm is another useful skill. You can use a piece of cloth or a bandana to create a sling. The first responder can help the injured friend put it on and make sure the arm is supported. Recognizing and treating signs of dehydration is also important. Your friend can pretend to feel dizzy and have a dry mouth. The first responder can offer water and guide them to a shaded area to rest.

To conduct these role-playing scenarios, you need to set up the scene with props and first aid supplies. Use items like bandages, wet wipes, tweezers, and a piece of cloth for the sling. You can create a simple first-aid kit with these supplies. Start by explaining the scenario to everyone involved. Make sure everyone understands their role. Guide the kids through the steps of first aid treatment. For example, if someone is treating a cut, remind them to clean the wound first, apply an antiseptic, and finally put on a bandage. Encourage everyone to take turns being the injured person and the first responder. This way, everyone gets a chance to practice different skills.

Role-playing has many learning benefits. It allows you to practice hands-on techniques in a safe environment. You can make mistakes and learn from them without any real danger. This helps build confidence in your ability to respond to real-life situations. When you practice these skills, they become second nature. You'll know what to do without having to think too hard. This quick response can be crucial in an emergency. Role-playing also helps you stay calm under pressure. You'll feel more prepared and less likely to panic when you've practiced a scenario many times.

Let's look at some tips for making the role-playing sessions more effective. First, make the scenarios as realistic as possible. Use props and act out the situations to make them feel real. Second, encourage everyone to ask questions. If someone is unsure about a step, they should feel comfortable asking for help. Third, give feedback after each scenario. Talk about what went well and what could be improved. This helps everyone learn and get better. Finally, have fun! Role-playing is a great way to learn, but it should also be enjoyable. Laughing and having a good time make the practice more memorable.

You'll be better prepared for real-life situations by practicing first aid through role-playing. You'll know how to treat cuts, handle insect bites, use a sling, and recognize dehydration. These skills are important for keeping yourself and others safe. So, gather your friends, set up your props, and start practicing. You'll have fun and learn valuable skills that could make a big difference one day.

NAVIGATION CHALLENGES WITH MAPS AND COMPASSES

Imagine you're out in the woods with a group of friends, and you need to find your way back to camp. You have a map and a compass, but you're not sure how to use them together. A navigation challenge can help you practice these skills in a fun and exciting way. You'll set up a course with different checkpoints, each marked on a map. At each checkpoint, you'll find a clue or a task to complete. This helps you learn how to read a map, use a compass, and make good decisions.

First, you'll need some materials for the navigation challenge. You'll need topographic maps of the area where you're practicing. These maps show important details like hills, rivers, and paths. You'll also need compasses for each participant or team. A compass helps you find directions like North, South, East, and West. Having both a map and a compass will guide you through the course. Make sure everyone has a way to carry their map and compass, like a small backpack or a pocket.

To organize the navigation course, start by marking checkpoints on the map. These are specific spots you need to visit. You can mark them with a pen or a sticker. Next, go into the field and mark these checkpoints with something noticeable. You could use colored flags, ribbons, or even small signs. At each checkpoint, leave a clue or task for the participants. For example, you might ask them to identify a type of tree or find a small hidden object. These tasks make the challenge more interactive and fun.

Here's a step-by-step guide to setting up the challenge. First, choose a safe and interesting area for the course. Make sure it's a place where you can easily supervise the participants. Next, create a simple map with clear checkpoints. Mark these checkpoints in the real world using flags or ribbons. Then, come up with clues or tasks for each checkpoint. Write these down and leave them at the checkpoints. Finally, give each participant or team their map and compass. Explain the rules and let them start the challenge.

This navigation challenge teaches many valuable lessons. You'll practice reading maps and using compasses in a real-world setting. This helps you understand how to navigate through different terrains. You'll also enhance your problem-solving and decision-making skills. Each checkpoint presents a new challenge; you'll need to think carefully to complete it. Working in teams encourages collaboration and communication, which are important in any survival situation.

By participating in a navigation challenge, you'll gain confidence in your ability to find your way. You'll learn to trust your tools and your instincts. The skills you practice will not only help you in the wild but also in everyday life. Whether you're exploring a new park, hiking a trail, or just finding your way around, these navigation skills will come in handy.

So grab your maps, compasses, and friends. Set up a course, mark your checkpoints, and get ready for an adventure. You'll have fun, learn a lot, and become a better navigator. Enjoy the thrill of finding your way and discovering new places.

CREATING YOUR OWN SURVIVAL JOURNAL

Keeping a survival journal is like creating your own adventure book. It helps you track your progress and look back on what you've learned. You can record experiences and observations, making remembering important details easier. Every time you practice a survival skill, you can write it down. This helps you see how much you've improved. Documenting your activities and lessons can be fun and rewarding. You can include drawings and diagrams of things like shelters you've built, plants you've identified, or navigation routes you've taken. This makes your journal more interesting and easier to understand.

Starting your survival journal is easy and fun. Begin with daily entries of what you did and what you learned. Write about the activities you tried and how they went. Include details like what worked well and what didn't. Adding drawings and diagrams can help you visualize your experiences. For example, if you built a shelter, draw a picture of it and label the different parts. If you identified a plant, sketch its leaves and flowers. You can also reflect on challenges and successes. Write about what was difficult and how you overcame it. This helps you think about what you learned and how you can improve next time.

Making your journal engaging and personal is important. You can add photos or sketches of your outdoor adventures. Take pictures of the shelters you built or the plants you found and paste them into your journal. If you enjoy drawing, sketch scenes from your experiences. You can also include pressed leaves or flowers that you found during foraging. This adds a special touch to your journal and makes it unique. You can decorate the pages with stickers, colorful pens, or anything else that makes you happy. This creativity makes your journal something you'll want to look at again and again.

Keeping a survival journal has many benefits. It encourages reflection and critical thinking. By writing about your experiences, you can think deeply about what you learned. This helps reinforce the skills you've practiced. Your journal also serves as a personal record of your outdoor experiences and achievements. You can look back and see how much you've grown. It's like having a book that tells the story of your adventures. This can motivate and make you feel proud of what you've accomplished.

A survival journal is more than just a book. It's a way to capture your adventures and learn from them. Every entry, drawing, and pressed leaf tells a part of your story. It helps you remember the skills you practiced and the fun you had. By keeping a journal, you create a keepsake that you can look back on for years to come. It's a great way to stay connected to your experiences and continue learning. So grab a notebook and some pens, and start your survival journal today. You'll enjoy making it and treasure it for a long time.

KEEPING THE ADVENTURE ALIVE

Now that you have everything you need to explore the outdoors and use your new survival skills, it's time to share your knowledge and help other kids find the same excitement.

Simply by leaving your honest opinion of this book on Amazon, you'll show other young adventurers where they can find the information they're looking for, and pass your passion for outdoor survival skills forward.

Thank you for your help. The spirit of adventure stays alive when we share what we've learned—and you're helping me to do just that.

Scan the QR code to leave your review on Amazon.

Leave a Review

CONCLUSION

You've reached the end of an incredible journey. Let's take a moment to look back at everything we've covered in this book.

Chapter 1 started with the basics of outdoor survival, emphasizing the importance of preparation and planning. We covered essential survival gear, talked about how to create a personalized bug-out bag, and highlighted the importance of maintaining your bug-out bag to ensure readiness for any situation.

In Chapter 2, we moved on to safety in the wilderness. We talked about how to handle common problems, like minor cuts or scrapes, insect bites, sprained ankles, sunburns, and dehydration. We covered how to take necessary precautions and signal for help in emergencies, and we highlighted the importance of staying calm in challenging situations to think clearly and make the best decisions.

In Chapter 3, we explored essential fire-making techniques, starting with the basics of fire safety. Fire safety is so important that I'm going to put the fire safety checklist here, too:

- Do you have adult supervision or the help of another person?
- Have you picked a safe location with ground that is bare or covered with rocks?
- Do you have a fire blanket, sand, or water to put out the fire?
- Will the weather conditions, like high winds and dry leaves, cause your fire to spread out of control?

We discussed how to collect and prepare tinder and kindling for an effective fire setup and covered specific fire-starting methods, such as using a magnifying glass or flint and steel.

In Chapter 4, we focused on shelter-building techniques in the wilderness, starting with how to select a safe and suitable shelter site. We covered how to build different types of shelters, including a lean-to, a debris hut, and a tarp shelter, using either natural materials or what you have in your bug-out bag.

In Chapter 5, we discussed how to obtain safe drinking water in the wilderness by collecting rainwater or finding lakes, streams, or natural springs. We covered effective techniques for collecting water while minimizing contamination risks. We also explored two key methods for purifying water: boiling and using purification tablets, which ensure water is safe for consumption in survival situations.

Chapter 6 discussed the basics of foraging and how to safely find and identify edible plants in the wilderness. We covered rules for foraging, such as ensuring plants are safe to eat by recognizing common edible species. We also covered avoiding poisonous plants and highlighted safe foraging practices to prevent illness or injury while exploring nature.

In Chapter 7, we focused on developing navigational skills essential for outdoor survival. We started with the basics of reading a map and using a compass to stay oriented. Then, we talked about natural navigation techniques, such as using the sun and stars to find direction. Finally, we talked about how to create simple trail markers to help keep track of your path in unfamiliar terrain.

Chapter 8 explored how to read and interpret weather in the wilderness by understanding cloud formations and weather patterns. We covered how to predict changes in weather using natural signs to anticipate conditions like rain or storms. We also discussed practical tips on preparing for adverse weather and staying safe in extreme conditions, such as heatwaves, extreme cold, and lightning storms.

Chapter 9 focused on developing a strong survival mindset and resilience in the wilderness. We highlighted the importance of staying calm under pressure and building confidence and self-reliance to handle tough situations. We also reviewed some strategies for effective problem-solving in challenging environments, staying motivated when faced with difficult conditions, and maintaining a positive outlook and perseverance in survival scenarios.

In Chapter 10 we recounted real-life survival stories. These stories showed how important the skills in this book are and how to use multiple skills together to survive.

Finally, in Chapter 11, you have some fun activities to practice your skills, like scavenger hunts and building miniature shelters.

So, what are the key takeaways from this book? First, always stay calm and think clearly. Second, know how to find shelter, water, and food. Third, practice your navigation skills. And finally, always be prepared and stay safe.

Now, it's time for you to take action. Go out and practice these skills. Go on hikes with your family or friends. Try building a shelter in your backyard. Set up a scavenger hunt to test your foraging skills. The more you practice, the more confident you'll become.

Remember, the skills you've learned in this book are not just for emergencies. They help you connect with nature and feel more independent. You can use them to have fun and stay safe during your outdoor adventures.

You have the knowledge and the skills to handle any situation. You are prepared, confident, and ready for whatever comes your way. Nature is full of surprises, both fun and challenging. With your new skills, you can face these challenges and enjoy the beauty of the outdoors.

So go ahead, explore, learn, and have fun. The wilderness is waiting for you. And always remember, you are capable and strong. You have everything you need to survive and thrive in the wild. Keep practicing, stay curious, and never stop learning. The adventure is just beginning!

REFERENCES

AlertFind. (n.d.). *Storm and emergency safety guide for kids*. AlertFind. https://alertfind.com/storm-and-emergency-safety-guide-for-kids/

All Terrain Outdoors. (n.d.). *What equipment do you need for outdoor theater/movie nights?*. https://www.all-terrainoutdoors.com/what-equipment-do-you-need-for-outdoor-theater-movie-nights/

Art of Manliness. (n.d.). *The ultimate army field guide to wild edible plants*. Art of Manliness. https://www.artofmanliness.com/skills/outdoor-survival/wild-edible-plants/

Barley & Birch. (n.d.). *14 low-prep outdoor scavenger hunt ideas for kids*. Barley & Birch. https://barleyandbirch.com/discover-simple-outdoor-scavenger-hunt-ideas-for-kids/

Battlbox. (n.d.). *The art of fire making: Traditional vs modern techniques*. Battlbox.com. https://www.battlbox.com/blogs/battlbox/the-art-of-fire-making-traditional-vs-modern-techniques

Big Life Journal. (n.d.). *How to teach problem-solving to children and preteens*. Big Life Journal. https://biglifejournal.com/blogs/blog/how-teach-problem-solving-strategies-kids-guide?

Boosa Tech. (n.d.). *Dressing for success on the slopes: What to wear under ski pants*. https://boosatech.com/blogs/news/dressing-for-success-on-the-slopes-what-to-wear-under-ski-pants

British Red Cross. (n.d.). *Practise first aid skills*. British Red Cross. https://firstaidchampions.redcross.org.uk/en/primary/first-aid-skills/practise-first-aid-skills/

The Bug Out Bag Guide. (n.d.). *Primitive fire making: 6 ways to make fire without matches*. The Bug Out Bag Guide. https://www.thebugoutbagguide.com/primitive-fire-making/

Burke, M. (2016). *Strategy implementation insights from the Competition Commission South Africa*. https://core.ac.uk/download/188771763.pdf

Campsited. (n.d.). *Camping in the rain with kids: Tips and tricks*. Campsited. https://www.campsited.com/en/blog/camping-in-the-rain-with-kids-tips-and-tricks/

Centers for Disease Control and Prevention. (n.d.). *Helping children cope with emergencies*. CDC. https://www.cdc.gov/childrenindisasters/helping-children-cope.html

Centers for Disease Control and Prevention. (n.d.). *Water treatment options when hiking, camping, or traveling.* CDC. https://www.cdc.gov/healthywater/drinking/travel/index.html

Empowering Parents. (n.d.). *How to motivate the unmotivated child.* Empowering Parents. https://www.empoweringparents.com/article/motivating-the-unmotivated-child/

EST Gear. (n.d.). *The importance of safety and creating a survival shelter.* EST Gear. https://estgear.com/blog/the-importance-of-safety-and-creating-a-survival-shelter?

First Aid Darwin. (n.d.). *Emergency first aid for natural disasters.* First Aid Darwin. https://firstaidcoursesdarwin.com.au/blog/emergency-first-aid-for-natural-disasters/

Flying Deer Nature Center. (n.d.). *How to build a debris hut.* Flying Deer Nature Center. https://flyingdeernaturecenter.org/how-to-build-a-debris-hut/#:

Fox 13 News. (n.d.). *Boy survives 24 hours alone in Arizona desert after he wandered from his home.* Fox 13 News. https://www.fox13news.com/news/boy-survives-24-hours-alone-in-arizona-desert-after-he-wandered-from-his-home

From Tent to Takeoff. (n.d.). *Camping survival kit for kids - 13 essential items.* From Tent to Takeoff. https://fromtenttotakeoff.com/camping-survival-kit-for-kids/KOA. (n.d.). *Top 8 outdoor skills for youth.*

The Fun Outdoors. (n.d.). *How to use a compass without a map.* https://thefunoutdoors.com/survival/how-to-use-compass-without-map/

Garden and Health. (n.d.). *Using social media to spread the joy of foraging.* https://garden-and-health.com/using-social-media-to-spread-the-joy-of-foraging/

Green Pest Defense. (2023, April 23). *Tick prevention tips: How to protect yourself and your family from ticks.* Green Pest Defense. https://greenpestdefense.com/2023/04/23/tick-prevention-tips-how/

Guidinguk. (2023, November 11). *Kasım 11, 2023.* https://www.guidinguk.com/2023/11/11/

Healthline. (n.d.). *Poison sumac: Rash, pictures, and treatment.* https://www.healthline.com/health/outdoor-health/poison-sumac?utm_source=ReadNext

HowStuffWorks. (n.d.). *10 ways animals supposedly predict the weather.* HowStuffWorks. https://science.howstuffworks.com/nature/climate-weather/storms/10-ways-animals-supposedly-predict-the-weather.htm

Infection Cycle. (n.d.). *Can an infected wound heal without treatment?.* Infection Cycle. https://infectioncycle.com/articles/can-an-infected-wound-heal-without-medical-intervention-signs-risks-and-treatment-options

Insights Success. (n.d.). *Tips to embrace discipline and make the most out of the year.* Insights Success. https://www.insightssuccess.in/web-stories/tips-to-embrace-discipline-and-make-the-most-out-of-the-year/

Junior Leadership. (n.d.). *Emergencies can happen at any time.* https://www.juniorlead ership.net/post/emergencies-can-happen-at-any-time

Kids On The Land. (n.d.). *Activity #5 KOL – Using your 5 senses on a nature scavenger hunt.* https://kidsontheland.org/activity-5-kol-using-your-5-senses-on-a-nature-scavenger-hunt/

KOA Blog. https://koa.com/blog/top-outdoor-skills-for-youth/

Little Passports. (n.d.). *How to use a compass and read a map.* Little Passports. https://www.littlepassports.com/blog/educational/use-compass-read-map/?srsltid= AfmBOorzNVMZzYdRG6_YW34z7I0LS_6QeeqQbHDeVgrDHdVhtC5BlKoq

Mallorca Sailing. (n.d.). *Navigating the stars: A beginner's guide to celestial navigation.* Mallorca Sailing. https://www.mallorcasailing.com/articles/navigating-the-stars-a-beginners-guide-to-celestial-navigation

MasterClass. (n.d.). *How to find water: 5 ways to collect safe drinking water.* MasterClass. https://www.masterclass.com/articles/how-to-find-water

MasterClass. (n.d.). *Lean-to shelters: How to build a lean-to shelter in the wild.* MasterClass. https://www.masterclass.com/articles/lean-to-shelter

Men's Journal. (n.d.). *Bushcraft: How to start a fire with flint and steel.* Men's Journal. https://www.mensjournal.com/adventure/bushcraft-how-to-start-a-fire-with-flint-and-steel

Mind Body Thrive. (n.d.). *Overcoming the perfectionism trap.* https://www.mind bodythrive.com/blog/overcoming-the-perfectionism-trap

Miracle Renata. (n.d.). *The power of self-belief: Building confidence for success.* https://www.miraclerenata.com/post/the-power-of-self-belief-building-confidence-for-success

The MMOB. (n.d.). *How to prepare yourself for an international adventure.* https://www.themmob.org/self-care-checklist-before-a-trip-abroad/

National Geographic Education. (n.d.). *Map skills for students.* National Geographic Education. https://education.nationalgeographic.org/resource/map-skills-for-students/

NBC News. (2023). *How 4 children survived 40 days in the Amazon jungle after a plane crash.* NBC News. https://www.nbcnews.com/news/world/how-4-children-survived-40-days-jungle-plane-crash-amazon-colombia-rcna88791

O'Donoghue, T. (n.d.). *A quick trip around the winter sky.* http://www.trevorodonoghue.com/a-quick-trip-around-the-winter-sky/

Orlando Science Center. (n.d.). *Outdoor safety for kids: 7 survival tips for any scenario.* Orlando Science Center. https://www.osc.org/outdoor-survival-for-kids-7-safety-tips-for-any-scenario/

Pew Pew Tactical. (n.d.). *DIY survival shelters: How to build a shelter with no tools.* Pew Pew Tactical. https://www.pewpewtactical.com/diy-survival-shelters/

The Prepared. (n.d.). *How to read maps.* https://theprepared.com/survival-skills/guides/maps-101/

Raising Children. (n.d.). *Dangerous plants: Keeping children safe.* Raising Children. https://raisingchildren.net.au/toddlers/safety/poisons/dangerous-plants

REI. (n.d.). *How to use a compass: Compass/map navigation.* REI. https://www.rei.com/learn/expert-advice/navigation-basics.html?

REI. (n.d.). *Wilderness first aid basics: Expert advice.* REI. https://www.rei.com/learn/expert-advice/wilderness-first-aid-basics.html?

Run Wild My Child. (n.d.). *Teaching map reading skills to kids: Toddlers thru teens.* Run Wild My Child. https://runwildmychild.com/map-reading-skills/

Scaffolded Math and Science. (2018, February). *A step-by-step guide to scavenger hunts {and a free percents scavenger hunt}.* https://www.scaffoldedmath.com/2018/02/percents-scavenger-hunt.html

Scouting Magazine. (2019, February). *Signaling for help in the wilderness.* Scouting Magazine. https://scoutingmagazine.org/2019/02/signaling-for-help-in-the-wilderness/

Sigma 3 Survival School. (n.d.). *Best natural fire tinder.* Sigma 3 Survival School. https://survivalschool.us/best-natural-fire-tinder/

Slidetodoc. (n.d.). *Introduction to weather and meteorology.* https://slidetodoc.com/introduction-to-weather-and-meteorology-rangi-weather-and/

Survival Gear. (n.d.). *2012 survival kit - plan ahead.* https://www.survival-gear.com/articles/2012-survival-kit-plan-ahead-just-in-case/

Survival Sherpa. (n.d.). *Spontaneous combustion.* Survival Sherpa. https://survivalsherpa.wordpress.com/tag/spontaneous-combustion/

Survival Skill Zone. (n.d.). *Essential wilderness survival skills.* Survival Skill Zone. https://survivalskillzone.com/essential-wilderness-survival-skills/

Survival Skill Zone. (n.d.). *How to deal with common skin conditions in the wilderness.* Survival Skill Zone. https://survivalskillzone.com/how-to-deal-with-common-skin-conditions-in-the-wilderness/

The Survival University. (n.d.). *Survival psychology and creating a survivalist mindset.* The Survival University. https://thesurvivaluniversity.com/survival-tips/understanding-survival-psychology-to-create-a-strong-survivalist-mindset

TeachEngineering. (n.d.). *The water around us - Activity.* TeachEngineering. https://www.teachengineering.org/activities/view/rice2-2526-water-natural-source-freshwater-saltwater-activity#:

Texas Bushcraft. (n.d.). *Creating and using trail markers in the wild.* Texas Bushcraft. https://www.texasbushcraft.com/blogs/news/creating-and-using-trail-markers-in-the-wild#:

Thrifty Hiker. (n.d.). *A guide to tarp shelter configurations.* Thrifty Hiker. https://thriftyhiker.com/a-guide-to-tarp-shelter-configurations/

Total Health Care. (n.d.). *Berries & nuts: The antioxidant super duo*. https://www.total-health-care.com/berries-nuts-the-antioxidant-super-duo/

TruePrepper. (2024). *Kids' bug out bag list: 14 essentials for 2024*. TruePrepper. https://trueprepper.com/kids-bug-out-bag/

U.S. Environmental Protection Agency. (n.d.). *Emergency disinfection of drinking water*. EPA. https://www.epa.gov/ground-water-and-drinking-water/emergency-disinfection-drinking-water

U.S. Fire Administration. (n.d.). *Fire safety for children*. U.S. Department of Homeland Security. https://www.usfa.fema.gov/prevention/home-fires/at-risk-audiences/children/

Vocal. (n.d.). *Camping in the winter: How to enjoy the outdoors even in the cold*. Families. https://vocal.media/families/camping-in-the-winter-how-to-enjoy-the-outdoors-even-in-the-cold

Weather Wiz Kids. (n.d.). *Cloud types*. Weather Wiz Kids. https://www.weatherwizkids.com/weather-clouds.htm

Westminster Outdoor Living. (n.d.). *June is National Camping Month!*. https://www.westminsteroutdoorliving.com/Catalogue/about-us/media/Blogs/June-is-National-Camping-Month

WhiteClouds. (n.d.). *Vicinity maps*. https://www.whiteclouds.com/3dpedia/vicinity-maps/

wikiHow. (n.d.). *How to start a fire with just a magnifying glass*. wikiHow. https://www.wikihow.com/Create-Fire-With-a-Magnifying-Glass

Wilder Child. (n.d.). *A beginners guide to foraging for wild edibles with kids*. Wilder Child. https://wilderchild.com/blogs/news/foraging-for-wild-edibles-with-kids

Wildlings Forest School. (n.d.). *The benefits of teaching your kids bushcraft and survival*. Wildlings Forest School. https://www.wildlingsforestschool.com/blog/bushcraft-and-survival-life-skills

Windsor-Essex County Health Unit. (n.d.). *Winter storm*. https://www.wechu.org/emergency-preparedness/winter-storm

Made in United States
Orlando, FL
05 November 2024

53496175R00067